Plays
by
Steve
Carter

357 W 20th St., NY NY 10011
212 627-1055

Plays by Steve Carter

First printing: December 1986

ISBN: 0-88145-043-X

Design by Marie Donovan
Set in Aster by L&F Technical Composition, Lakeland, FL
Printed on acid-free paper and bound by BookCrafters, Inc., Chelsea, MI

Contents

Having seen *Dame Lorraine, House of Shadows,* and *One Last Look,* and having performed as an actor in *Eden* and *Nevis Mountain Dew,* I'm thoroughly convinced that Steve Carter is one of the top writers in the country. I had the rare privilege of studying playwriting in Steve Carter's Workshop at the Negro Ensemble Company, and I say with conviction that no single individual has influenced my writing to the degree that Steve Carter has. Bravo Steve Carter! Bravo!

Samm-Art Williams

About the Author

steve carter, Playwright, was born, raised, and still (despite extensive travel and various residences) lives in New York City.

He has written some twenty-six plays that he keeps securely out of sight and circulation, hidden in a trunk. Perhaps some future generation will uproot them and laugh along with him.

Among those to which he'll presently own up are *Eden* and *Nevis Mountain Dew*, written in 1975 and 1977, respectively. These two plays, along with *Dame Lorraine* (written in 1979), comprise his "Caribbean Trilogy". He is also the author of *Primary Colors* and *Terraces* (developed from his shorter play, *The Terraced Apartment*).

Filming begins shortly on the film, *A Time Called Eden*, based on *Eden*, and for which he wrote the screenplay.

He is a recipient of Creative Writing Fellowships from the Guggenheim and Rockefeller Foundations, as well as the National Endowment for the Arts. A member of the prestigious New Dramatists since July 1981, he is also a MacDowell Fellow.

From 1968 to 1981 Carter was a member of the Negro Ensemble Company where he worked in a variety of capacities, including Playwright-in-Residence, a position he now enjoys with Chicago's Victory Gardens Theater. It is at this theatre that a new musical, *Shoot Me While I'm Happy*, for which he's written the book, will open in November, 1986.

He is a Scorpio and confesses to the sin of pride when it comes to his prowess in the kitchen: "I am a pretty fair cook!"

He is dedicated to life in the American Regional Theatre and believes that the only fit way to end any current "bio" is . . . "I am currently at work on a new play!"

House of Shadows

House of Shadows was first produced at the Victory Gardens Theater in Chicago on 1 April 1982 (title: *Shadows*). Chuck Smith directed the following cast:

ERIC . . . . Rodrick Wimberly
CASSIE . . . . Letitia Toole
MARY . . . . Shirley Spiegler Jacobs
HECTOR . . . . Butch Williams

Patrick Kerwin designed the set; Kate Bergh, the costumes; Robert Christen, the lighting; and Galen C. Ramsey, the sound.

House of Shadows was recently produced by the Negro Ensemble Company in New York City on 16 January 1986. Clinton Turner Davis directed the following cast:

ERIC . . . . Teddy Abner
CASSIE . . . . Frances Foster
AARON . . . . Daniel Barton
HECTOR . . . . Raymond Rosario
MARY . . . . Joan Grant
MAJESKI . . . . Victor Steinbach

Author's Note(s)

House of Shadows was written to display the talents of . . . as the French would say . . . "deux femmes du certaine age". It is my belief that mature and experienced character actressses can . . . vocally and by their attitude . . . transcend time and be younger when CASSIE and MARY must be so.

If I had my "druthers", I'd prefer AARON and MAJESKI to never come into physical contact with CASSIE or MARY.

The life-sized portrait of MAJESKI should be painted on scrim and the actor playing him . . . placed in a space behind it. Only when the lights come on behind the scrim should the actor be visible to the audience.

House of Shadows is dedicated:

To Aubrey, Judy, Jessica, Georgia, and Susan Greenberg,
with grateful thanks for opening their home to artists

and with grateful thanks

To Frances Foster, "La Doyenne de la Theatre Noir"—
You bring my plays to life. . .

Characters

CASSIE	Black female, approaching 80
MARY MAJESKI	White female, approaching 80
ERIC	Black male, 10
HECTOR	White-appearing, Latino male, 10

and

WLADEK MAJESKI

and

AARON SHAW

(*The set is, for the most part, skeletal and murky. It needn't be totally realistic as long as it gives the feeling that this was once a good house in a formerly grand neighborhood. Essential to the set are the door to* MARY's *room (formerly the maid's room), a door to the kitchen, a staircase that leads upstairs to an unseen second landing, and a fireplace, over which hangs the life-sized portrait of a stiffly posed, robust, white man in his early fifties. The place fairly bursts at the seams with old furniture, curios, doo-dads, what-nots, etc. Also essential are an outside area, overrun by weeds and ivy, and an entrance to the side of the house. In the darkness we hear an almost inaudible sobbing. The lights ease up slightly to reveal a young, black boy nervously pacing the area outside the house. The sound of the sobbing continues. The lights on the exterior go down and those on the interior come up.* CASSIE *comes in from the kitchen carrying a tray. She stops in front of the portrait.*)

CASSIE: Well . . . what you got planned for today, Mr. Bastard?

(CASSIE *walks toward the door from whence the crying comes. As she puts her hands on the knob, the sobbing stops. She goes inside and comes, almost immediately, out—without the tray. As she shuts the door behind herself, the faint sobbing starts up again.* CASSIE, *once again, comes before the portrait which seems to glow and have a transparency at the same time.*)

CASSIE: Is this it? Is it gonna be today?

(*As* CASSIE *contemplates the portrait, an eerie light seems to play on the staircase. Dimly, the figure of a male, more a presence than anything real, can be made out.*)

AARON: Cassie! Cassie!

CASSIE: Go 'way! Go 'way!

AARON: Cassie. Sweet, sweet Cassie.

CASSIE: 'Way! 'Way from me, Aaron Shaw! Got no time for you today. 'Way from me, Devil Aaron.

AARON: Sweet Cassie.

CASSIE: "Sweet Cassie", my hind parts! Go'way! Ain't gonna say it no more.

(Laughing softly, the figure fades. The errie light goes out. CASSIE *slowly makes her way up the stairs. In the half-light, the black boy still fidgets.)*

ERIC: Damn!

(As CASSIE *gets to the top of the stairs, a loud crash of glass and china being hurled to the floor is heard.* CASSIE *starts back down angrily.)*

CASSIE: Unh-unh! Not on your life! Not this day! Damn heifer! One! Two! Three! Think I'm some damn slave? Think I'm some damn slave pickin' up after your behind? Four! Five! Never happen! Six! Seven! Think you still some damn princess and I'm your slave? Eight! That mess can stay right where you threw it, for all I care. It can stay right there 'till it rot and smell like you! Nine! Not today, Honey! Not today! Ten! There! Don't get me mad again. Don't make me have to come in there and do something to you. You hear me, heifer? You hear me? All right now!

(She stands there ... a little bewildered.)

What was I doing? Damn heifer's always making me forget what I was doing. Old Cow! You better not make me mad this day. When I come in there you better have all that mess cleaned up. Wasn't nothing wrong with that food. You ain't had no cause to pitch it on the floor like that. Who you think you are, hunh? Who you think you are?

*(*CASSIE *goes into the room. It is obvious from her manner of speaking that she is straining and picking up the broken things.)*

Still think you too good, don't you, Miss High and Messy? Still think you better than everybody else, don't you? Well, I'm here to tell you, "you ain't!" You pitch food that I slave so hard to fix ... one more time ... and I'm gonna let you starve to death from here on in. You hear? I don't care whether "The Master" like it or not I ain't fixin' nothing else. You got that? Nothing else! Just do it one more time and see if I don't mean what I say. See if I don't just let your old, wrinkled up behind starve to death.

(She comes out of the room carrying the tray with the broken things and the picked-up food.)

You ought to die anyway. You sure ain't doing anybody no good 'round here with your old, ugly self. Old, messy woman! You hear that? OLD ... MESSY ... WOMAN! You ought to die. One of us ought to die. I ought to die first ... just to spite you ... *(To the portrait)* ... and you!

(She goes off into the kitchen. Sobbing is heard from the room. CASSIE *returns and is about to mount the stairs.)*

Stop that! Stop that noise! You know I don't like it! Stop it! You hear me? Stop it! I can't stand it and you know it! If you don't stop, I'm gonna go upstairs and close my door so I can't hear you!

(*The sobbing continues—slightly louder.*)

I'm gonna do it. I ain't foolin'!

(*The sobbing continues.*)

I'm going!

(*The sobbing continues.*)

I'm on the stairs . . .

(*The sobbing continues.* Cassie *climbs the stairs as fast as she can, mumbling all the way. Finally we hear a door slam. After a short beat,* Cassie *comes to the head of the stairs.*)

See? I told you I'd do it. Told you I'd go into my room and shut my door and not pay you no mind. You know I don't fool around. You know I mean what I say. Now, stop that damn noise!

(*The sobbing explodes into outright bawling.*)

Damn it! You makin' me mad again. You know I ain't supposed to get mad. One! Two! Three! Stop it! Four! Five! Stop it! Stop it! Six! Seven! Stop it! Stop it! Please! Eight? Please? Please? Nine?

Mary: (*Screaming from within.*) PAPA! PAPA! COME FOR ME! HELP ME! HELP ME, PAPA! I'M SORRY! I'M SORRY!

Cassie: Please . . .?

Mary: You punish me too long, Papa. Too long. Forgive me. Come and get me. Please, come and get me.

Cassie: I wish you would come. I wish you would come and get her and take her back to wherever the hell you comin' from. Then both of you would be out of my life for good . . .

(*The shadowy figure of* Aaron *appears and his low laughter is heard.*)

You come, too! I don't care. Both of y'all can come and get her. I want all three of you out of my life!

(Mary's *screaming continues.*)

Stop it!

(Cassie *runs into the room.*)

I begged you. I begged you to stop. I said, "Please".

(*The crying stops. The laughter stops.* CASSIE *comes out.*)

CASSIE: You heard me. I know you heard me. (*To the portrait*) You know she heard me. Oh, Lord, come and get me. Come quick, Lord. Please? It just ain't fair. What you do to people just ain't fair. You got me in this mess. Ain't nobody to blame but you, Lord. Nobody to blame . . . but you. Why you so mean to people? You make people suffer too long . . . way too long. Ain't nothing I done . . . so bad . . . I should have to suffer this long. People always talking 'bout how good you are, but they don't know you like I know you. You mean and spiteful and . . . you a devil . . .

(AARON's *laughter . . . is heard.*)

. . . and as for you . . . get the hell out of here.

(*LIGHTS*)

(*Outside the house,* ERIC *still waits nervously. A second figure, a boy his own age, sneaks up on him.*)

HECTOR: As the ghost said to the bumble bee, "Boo, Bee!"

ERIC: What the hell's wrong with you, man? Sneakin' up on a man like that . . .

(HECTOR *laughs.*)

Ain't nothin' funny. Where you been? Tell me, "Be there early!", and you late . . .

HECTOR: I ain't late.

ERIC: . . . and everybody looking at me all funny and everything . . .

HECTOR: Your imagination!

ERIC: . . . wonderin' what I'm doin' here and shit . . . and you takin' your sweet-ass time like you got all the time in the world . . .

HECTOR: Chill!

ERIC: Where you been, man?

HECTOR: I said, "Chill", Blood . . .

ERIC: "Chill", my ass! "Blood", my ass! Where you been?

HECTOR: "Man!"

ERIC: Man!

HECTOR: You got one short memory. I told you I had to go to Mass.

ERIC: I'm out here waitin' on your ass and you in church? On Friday?

HECTOR: Memorial Mass . . . for my Grandmother. Whole family was there. Some all the way from P.R., man. I told you, man . . .

ERIC: Ain't told me nothin'.

HECTOR: I told your ass. Ain't my fault you can't remember . . .

ERIC: . . . I'm out here takin' all the chances . . .

HECTOR: What chances?

ERIC: . . . and this dude in church.

HECTOR: That's where I was . . .

ERIC: But your grandma been dead . . .

HECTOR: A year . . . today. What you think a memorial Mass is, man? Man, I had to go. My papi would've broke my ass if I wasn't there. 'Sides . . . I ain't had no choice. My folks say, "Go!" . . . I go! All there is to it, man.

ERIC: Silly-ass custom . . . to me.

HECTOR: Well, what ain't silly to you?

ERIC: What you say?

HECTOR: You mouthin' off 'cause we got tradition . . . and you ain't.

ERIC: Tradition, my ass! You shoulda been here on time, that's all.

HECTOR: Look, man, did she come out yet?

ERIC: No!

HECTOR: Do she ever come out before now?

ERIC: Well . . .

HECTOR: How long I been checkin' this out now? Man, I know you nervous. I was nervous my first time, too. But damn, man . . . it ain't 'bout nothin'. You just got to get over the hump. Trust me. Would I be here at all if it wasn't a sure thing. Just trust ol' Hector and don't be so damn jumpy.

ERIC: Man, if anything go wrong and we get caught . . .

HECTOR: Man, look . . . if you gonna white out on me . . . hell . . . forget it. I can do this by my lonesome, you know. Damn! Try to do a friend a favor.

ERIC: Easy for you to say, man. Your brother ain't no cop.

HECTOR: So what? Just 'cause my brothers are in the Diablos, you think that make it easy on me. My brothers . . . 'specially 'Cardo . . . kick my ass 'round the block they find out I'm even thinkin' 'bout doin' this shit . . . never mind getting caught. Shit, crooked as the cops is, your brother get you off easy. Maybe slap you 'round some, but I bet he get you off. Shit, tonight's Friday. My brothers be 'round to the church at seven just to check. I ain't there for choir practice, they both go up side my head, man. That shit got to stop. In three years when I'm thirteen, they try messin' with me, I'm gonna mess them up . . . for good.

ERIC: All of that don't stop me from being . . .

HECTOR: Aw, man. Damn! Ain't nothin' gonna happen. Come on! We got time to get a Coke.

ERIC: You sure?

HECTOR: She ain't gonna do nothin' today she don't do every day. I ain't gonna say it no more. You want the Coke or not?

ERIC: You buying?

HECTOR: Shit, yeah!

ERIC: Let's go! Oh . . . one other thing . . .

HECTOR: What now?

ERIC: You got enough on you to spring for a Hostess Twinkie?

(*LIGHTS*)

(MARY, *dressed in faded finery and in a wheel chair, comes out of her room.*)

MARY: Breakfast!

(*Silence*)

I will take breakfast! Now!

(*Silence*)

Where is that girl? Cassie? Cassie? Cassie, I will have my breakfast now . . . and don't overcook my egg.

(*Silence*)

Cassie? Cassie! Come out here this instant, Cassie! Cassie? I know you're here. No sense playing childish games and pranks. I know you're here. Don't be a bad girl, Cassie. Oh, Lord, why are they so infantile. Don't be mean. Come out . . . now . . . and I won't be angry. But if you don't . . . If you don't . . . Well, I'm going to be angry. Very angry. Do you hear? Cassie? You didn't go out, did you? You know I don't like it when you go out without telling me. Come out, Cassie. I know you're here. You're here. You're just trying to frighten me. That's what you're doing, aren't you? You're just trying to scare me. Oh, you're such a bad girl. Bad, bad girl. Always trying to scare me. Well, I'm not going to be scared this time. I don't feel like humoring you. I don't feel like playing with you. There! You see? You've made me angry. Do you hear that, Cassie? I am angry with you. I am very angry with you. I am extremely angry with you. Cassie, please come out. I'm scared now. What did I do? Why are you mad with me? Did I do something wrong? Cassie? Cassie? I'm sorry. I won't toss my food away anymore. It was good food. You're a good cook, Cassie. I always said that. I always said to Papa, "Cassie's a good cook, Papa." I'm sorry. I'm sorry I hurt your feelings.

(CASSIE *comes out of her room and down the stairs.*)

You frightened me. You shouldn't . . . Don't frighten me like that. You see. You thought you could fool me. I knew you were here all the while. Trying to scare me. I wasn't scared, you know. Honestly, you people. You bad, bad girl. Did you think for one moment that you had me scared? Now, go and bring me my breakfast . . . and don't overcook my egg. In fact, I'm particularly ravenous today. I think I shall have two eggs . . . and don't you dare overcook either one of them. Do you hear me? Answer me!

(CASSIE *puts on hat, coat and gloves and leaves the stage.*)

Where are you going? Come back here!

(MARY *tries to follow her.*)

Don't you dare leave me when I'm talking to you. Come back here! You know I can't get through there. Get back here, I say!

(*A door opens and slams.*)

Come back. Please, come back. Please? Alone! All alone! Oh, Papa, I'm all alone. You shouldn't have left me all alone. Come back and get me.

(*The portrait luminesces and becomes transparent. Behind it is the active figure of* WLADEK MAJESKI.)

MAJESKI: You break my heart, Daughter. You break the heart of your father.

MARY: I will not look at you. You must not look at me like that. Go away. I will not see you! I will not see you!

MAJESKI: You break the heart of your father . . . who loved only you . . .

(AARON's *laughter is heard.*)

I loved only you, little Maria.

MARY: God . . . help me.

(*LIGHTS*)

(*Lights up outside the house.*)

ERIC: But what if she do double back?

HECTOR: She ain't!

ERIC: But just suppose she do . . .?

HECTOR: She ain't!

ERIC: How the hell you know for sure?

HECTOR: I know! Now, stop buggin' me. 'Sides . . . if she do double back . . .

ERIC: Yeah . . .?

HECTOR: We off her!

ERIC: Aw, no! I ain't goin' for none of that shit!

HECTOR: Damn, man. Can't nobody even joke with you?

ERIC: "Killin'" talk ain' no joke, man.

HECTOR: Sometimes I think you ain't got no kind of sense.

ERIC: Don't like me no "killin'" talk.

HECTOR: I think we ought to call this whole thing to one damn screechin' halt. You ain't ready, man. I get somebody else or do it alone. It don't matter to me.

ERIC: No! Just don't jive 'round 'bout offin' nobody . . .

HECTOR: You shoulda knowed I was just jivin', man.

(CASSIE *comes out of the side door pulling her shopping cart.*)

ERIC: Shut up. Here she come.

HECTOR: And right on time just like I said. She don't never miss. This gonna be it.

ERIC: Shut up, man.

HECTOR: What for? She can't hear us. She ain't even thinkin' 'bout us. Lighten up . . . if you can . . . and be cool, fool.

ERIC: I wonder if she really crazy like everybody say.

HECTOR: Here it is the middle of August . . . you see a old woman all bundled up like it about to snow any minute . . . and he got to ask if she crazy. Man, you crazy to be askin'. Okay, now. Here she come. Cool!

(CASSIE *walks by them and off.*)

ERIC: See? What I tell you? She look right at me.

HECTOR: She ain't even turn her head. Now, just chill for ten minutes or so. Give her chance to get on her bus. This gonna be smooth. I can feel it. This gonna be real smooth.

ERIC: Well . . . you might be right. I hope you right.

HECTOR: Like takin' candy from a grownup. Come on. Let's watch her get on the bus. Just to be sure.

ERIC: Right . . .

HECTOR: Right!

(*LIGHTS*)

(*Lights up on the interior.* MARY *speaks in a quite young voice.*)

MARY: Why are you so nervous?

AARON: I'm just thinkin' I shouldn't be up here, Miss Mary, Ma'am.

MARY: You're up here because I called you up here. That's part of your job . . . to come . . . when I call you.

AARON: Your father said I was never to come into your room unless . . .

MARY: My father is not here. Cassie is not here. Don't tell me you're worried about Cassie. Big, strong boy like you?

AARON: Cassie's my woman, Ma'am.

MARY: What difference does that make?

AARON: Cassie's a good woman, Ma'am.

MARY: So am I. A very good woman. I am a very good woman.

AARON: Ain't doubtin' you, Ma'am.

MARY: You're trying to tell me you've not had another woman since you and Cassie've been together?

AARON: Not gonna tell you that, Ma'am.

MARY: You going to tell me you've never thought about having me?

AARON: Not gonna tell you that, Ma'am, but Cassie's my woman.

MARY: What's that got to do with the price of eggs. I want you.

AARON: Yes, Ma'am.

MARY: Stop it! Stop it with the "Yes, Ma'am. No, Ma'am". You don't worry about Cassie. You pick her up in two hours. It'll take my dressmaker at least that long. She can't leave there unless you pick her up. So we're alone. Quite alone! Just you and . . . wonder of wonders . . . me! Got the whole house to ourselves, we have. Come over here, now. Let's see what you people are supposed to be so famous for. Well? Two hours isn't a hell of a lot of time.

AARON: . . . but 'twill do . . . M'am.

(The two boys come into the yard.)

HECTOR: Okay, now. This is it. I'm only going to ask you one more 'gain . . . and that's it. I don't want to hear no more 'bout it . . . either way. You in?

ERIC: Yeah!

HECTOR: Don't jerk me 'round, now. There ain't no turnin' back.

ERIC: I said, "Okay" . . . didn't I?

HECTOR: Okay. Let's go. Easy. Take your time. No rush. No rush. Yeah . . .

MARY: Yes . . .

HECTOR AND MARY: . . . the whole house to ourselves . . .

(The two boys prepare to enter through the side door.)

AARON: What was that? You hear something?

MARY: No.

AARON: I heard something.

MARY: Don't be so damned jumpy. It's too early for him . . .

AARON: 'Tain't him I'm worried 'bout, Ma'am.

MARY: Well, it can't be her. I'm certainly not worried about her. You're just hearing things. It's nothing, I tell you.

AARON: I don't know . . .

MARY: It's nothing. The wind, perhaps.

AARON: All the same . . .

MARY: Okay. Okay. Pull yourself together and get back downstairs . . . but I tell you it's nothing. Go see for yourself, if you have to. You're no good to me if you can't be relaxed. That's funny, don't you think? You're no good if you can't be relaxed and you're no good . . . relaxed. I suppose the humor is lost on you.

(HECTOR *reveals a set of skeleton keys and starts trying them out on the door.*)

AARON: There! You hear it that time?

MARY: Ssssshhhh!

(*The portrait lights up.*)

MAJESKI: Maria? Maria, where are you?

MARY: Oh, my God. It's him. You get out of here! Get out of here, I tell you. Get out or I'll scream. He'll never believe you.

MAJESKI: Maria?

MARY: In my room, Father. Go! Get out! No! In the closet! In the closet and keep still.

MAJESKI: You are not well?

MARY: I'm fine, Father.

MAJESKI: You are lazy girl. In bed all day is not good!

MARY: That's what you think. Don't preach, Father. I stay in bed because there's nothing else to do . . .

MAJESKI: I spoil you, little girl. I give you too much.

MARY: Yes, Father.

MAJESKI: I give you anything. Everything you want . . .

MARY: Because you love me, Father. Do I not remind you of Mother?

MAJESKI: . . . everything you want . . .

MARY: Not quite everything . . .

MAJESKI: What? What you ever want that I have not give you.

MARY: If I told you what I really wanted . . . you'd go crazy . . .

MAJESKI: What you say?

MARY: I said I'll settle for another house. That's it! Buy me . . . my own house.

MAJESKI: This is your house! Your home! It comes to you . . . when I go.

MARY: This is my mother's house!

MAJESKI: You have no mother . . .

MARY: Okay, then. It's your house! I don't want it. It's too small. Everyone laughs at this house.

MAJESKI: This house is good house. Like any house around here. Is good house.

MARY: It's too small. Everything about it is too small. Every house around here is bigger . . . grander. We are the laughing stock. The house is too small. We're too small. That's why I stay in bed. I'm ashamed to go out. Our neighbors all laugh at us. They call you "The king of the Polish Sausage". You're just a butcher. Look at you. Still wearing your bloody apron. We're nothing . . . nothing.

MAJESKI: Is Polish sausage give you roof over you head. Is Polish sausage give you food in you stomach. Is Polish sausage give you fancy clothes in closet. Is Polish sausage let you stay in this bed when other girls have to work. Is Polish sausage give you everything you have. Is this butcher with bloody apron give you everything you have.

MARY: I want a bigger house. I want the biggest house . . . ever. We're nothing. Just pretenders.

MAJESKI: We move to a house more large, we are not pretenders?

MARY: We only have two servants to do everything . . .

MAJESKI: Two people to take care of two people. Is not enough?

MARY: I want a bigger house. I'll leave if you don't buy a bigger house. I swear . . . I'll leave.

MAJESKI: Just like you mother . . .

MARY: Yes . . .

MAJESKI: Is my fault. I spoil you. I do this to you. You are not good person. I do this to you.

MARY: But, you love me . . .

MAJESKI: You are my daughter.

MARY: I am that.

(HECTOR *fumbles with the keys at the door.*)

MAJESKI: I hear noise.

MARY: I don't hear anything . . .

MAJESKI: Someone is here with you?

MARY: Don't be silly, Father. Who could be here with me. It must be the wind.

(*The light on the portrait goes out.*)

ERIC: What in the hell kind of keys are them?

HECTOR: How'd you think we was going to get in? Blow down the door like the big bad wolf or like they do on TV? Gotta look natural, man. With these, I can open any door in Chicago.

ERIC: Where you get'em?

HECTOR: Ripped 'em off my brother. He think he lost 'em.

(*They go in.*)

MARY: It must be the wind. You're hearing things, you silly, old man. Silly, old Father. Silly, old father.

(*Offstage, the two youths bump into something, making a noise ...*)

Cassie?

HECTOR: Easy, man.

ERIC: I know. I know. Hey?

HECTOR: What?

ERIC: What we whisperin' for if ain't nobody home?

MARY: You see? I knew you'd come back home, Miss Cassie. Well, it's no use trying to make up with me. I am thoroughly displeased with you. Thoroughly displeased. I won't talk to you. There!

(*She wheels herself into her room and closes the door. After a beat or so,* ERIC *and* HECTOR *come onstage.*)

HECTOR: Wow! What I tell you? Look at this place! Look at all this shit! It's a gold mine.

ERIC: Look like a lotta junk to me. I got ol', junky shit like this at my house.

HECTOR: Okay. So we go rip off your house. Man, ain't you never seen real antiques before? That's what they call this stuff. Antiques! Antiques is worth a fortune. Probably got all kinds of money stashed in boxes and stuck up in the fireplace and shit ...

ERIC: Smell funny in here. Like a tomb.

HECTOR: What you know 'bout tombs, Simp?

ERIC: Man, you ain't got to call me no ...

HECTOR: Hey, look at this. What she doing with this picture? Wonder who he is?

ERIC: 'Cause she black, she can't have no picture of no white dude? Man, I don't like this place.

HECTOR: This is gonna be it, my man. Always hear my brothers talking 'bout "The Honey Pot". Always saying how when a place like this get tore down after some ol' lady die, they always be findin' a lotta bucks and stuff. Read 'bout it all the time. Always know this ol' thing had money. Bet she got shit stashed in every room. Man, it's our duty to find the shit before she die and the cops get it all!

ERIC: Guess so . . . but this place still give me the natural creeps.

HECTOR: Man, don't you go out on me!

ERIC: Got this weird feeling. I should . . . Man, maybe I oughta go outside and lay. She might come back.

HECTOR: And what if she do? She a old lady, man. How she gonna catch us, we decide to run right over her? Hunh? How she gonna catch us? I'm gonna check out upstairs. You look 'round down here.

ERIC: For what?

HECTOR: Money, fool! Little things we can carry. Rings! Jewels! Chains! Money, man! Damn!! I got to tell you everything?

ERIC: You ain't got to tell me nothin'. You know, I'm gettin' kinda tired you talkin' like you was . . .

HECTOR: Yeah! I feel it! This gonna be my biggest score, yet. Stash in every room. I can feel this one.

ERIC: Only thing I feel is this dude's eyes lookin' down on me . . .

HECTOR: Smile, boy. You gonna be rich. You gonna be able to buy all the Sergio Valente jeans and Adidas shit you want.

(HECTOR *goes upstairs.* ERIC *stares at the portrait.*)

ERIC: What you lookin' at, Blue Eyes?

(ERIC *goes to* MARY'S *door, finds it locked, and begins to search around. While his back is turned, the door opens . . . silently. In the dim light* MARY *does not immediately see* ERIC.)

MARY: I knew you'd be back . . .

(ERIC *and* MARY, *upon seeing each other, freeze for an instant. In that instant,* CASSIE, *appears in the outside area.* MARY *and* ERIC *scream, simultaneously:*)

ERIC: Who you, Lady?

MARY: Who are you?

(They are both terrified. ERIC cowers against a wall. MARY is frozen in her wheel chair. CASSIE walks slowly toward the house, pulling her empty shopping cart. HECTOR comes running down, a small gun in his hands.)

HECTOR: What's going down? Who's this? Who you, Lady?

MARY: What do you want? Who are you?

HECTOR: Shut the hell up! Who the hell is this?

ERIC: How the hell I'm suppose to know. She come outta that room. Scared the livin' shit outta me.

MARY: What do you want here? Who are you?

HECTOR: I said shut up. How she get here? She ain't suppose to be here.

ERIC: I ain't know nothin', man. Hey ... you packin'? You packin'? Where you get the piece, man?

HECTOR: Gotta think.

ERIC: You know I don't like them things. I'm gettin' the hell outta here ...

HECTOR: Shut up and stay still, Nigger!

ERIC: What you call me ...?

HECTOR: Don't let me have to do nothing to you, now. Just chill and let me think.

ERIC: Man, you call me ...

HECTOR: You got me nervous, man. All that screamin' and carryin' on and shit ... I'm sorry.

ERIC: "Sorry" don't cut shit. We gonna lock asses. Piece or no piece, my pop told me don't let nobody call me a nigger.

HECTOR: I'm sorry. Okay?

MARY: Please, don't hurt me. There's nothing here but old things. Take what you want ... only ... please ... don't hurt me.

ERIC: Shut up, Lady! Come on, man. Put down the piece and let's get it on!

HECTOR: I said I was sorry. We got somethin' else to think 'bout now. What we gonna do 'bout this?

ERIC: Is no my problem, mang!

HECTOR: Well, we can't go and leave all this. Shit, she in a wheel chair. What can she do? Get some rope. Somethin'!

ERIC: From where?

MARY: Don't hurt me.

HECTOR: How the hell I know? From somewhere! Tie her ass up so she can't roll nowhere. Shit! I'll go look. Watch her.

(HECTOR *goes into* MARY'S *room.*)

MARY: Don't hurt me, please . . .

ERIC: Keep quiet and won't nothin' happen to nobody . . .

(ERIC *walks toward her.*)

MARY: Don't touch me! Don't you put your hands on me!

(HECTOR *comes from the room with the belts from some bathrobes.*)

HECTOR: Here. Tie her up. She givin' you a hard time?

ERIC: I can handle it.

MARY: Don't you touch me . . .

ERIC: Aw, shut the hell up. (*He ties* MARY'S *hands behind her.*)

What she doin' here, anyway. Ain't nobody supposed to be livin' here 'cept that ol' lady? Who are you?

HECTOR: I swear, man, I never knew nobody else was in this house. You been casin' the place 'long with me. You ain't never hear nobody say nothin' 'bout nobody else livin' here.

ERIC: Hey! What if . . . Anybody else in this house? Hey, Lady, anybody else . . .

HECTOR: I don't think so . . .

ERIC: How you know? You the one thought was only one ol' lady in here.

HECTOR: Cause the rooms upstairs in mostly almost empty. Ain't no beds . . . no chairs . . . Just bits and pieces . . . Junk . . .

ERIC: You check 'em all?

HECTOR: Almost . . . then I heard all the noise . . .

(CASSIE *comes, dejectedly, to the side door.*)

ERIC: Let's go check it out.

MARY: Please, don't hurt me. There's nothing here . . .

ERIC: I'd feel better if this ol' lady's mouth was tied up.

HECTOR: I'll do it.

MARY: No. Please . . .

HECTOR: Aw, shut up!

(*He gags her, then wheels her into her room, leaving the door open.*)

Okay? And, hey man, if somethin' like this come up again . . . don't scream . . okay? Just lay cool till I can sneak up on 'em.

ERIC: Don't worry. I ain't doing nothin' like this again. This my last time.

HECTOR: Yeah. Yeah, I said the same thing, my first time out. Eric?

ERIC: Yeah?

HECTOR: You still mad? 'Bout what I. . . . You know.

ERIC: Let's go check the damn rooms . . .

HECTOR: I'm real sorry, man. No jive. My papi woulda kill me if he heard me say that word. He tell me never to use that word 'cause we got some morenos in the family. I mean . . . you know. Hey, tell you what. You can call me "Spic" one time. I mean, if you want. Go 'head. I ain't gonna be mad. Just one time, though.

ERIC: Where you get the piece, man?

HECTOR: I always carry it. Well . . . I only had it a few days. I saved up for it.

ERIC: Word?

HECTOR: Word! Man, if 'Cardo knew, he'd kill me.

ERIC: How come you ain't never told me?

HECTOR: I know you ain't like 'em.

ERIC: Come on. Let's check out the rest of them rooms.

HECTOR: Well?

ERIC: "Well," what?

HECTOR: You gonna call me, "Spic", or no?

ERIC: Come on, man. 'Sides, my pop say that that word don't hurt y'all half as much as "nigger" hurt us.

HECTOR: No shit? I ain't really know what it mean. I just hear my brothers say it all the time . . .

(*They go off upstairs.* CASSIE *comes into the house and into the area.*)

CASSIE: Lord! Lord! Lord! What's the world coming to? I just don't know. The whole world is going crazy, I guess. I ain't on the bus no more that five minutes ... some little boy ... some little colored boy ... grab my pocketbook. Just grabbed it. Snatched it right out my hand and jumped off the bus. Couldn't been more than eleven ... twelve ... if he was that old. A little child, Mary. A little child. I don't understand. He didn't look like he was old enough to be riding the bus without his mama. He snatch my bag and just ... just jump off the bus. Nobody even did anything. Didn't make a move to help. Happened so fast. A cute, colored child ... too. Look like a little black angel. Lord! Lord! Lord! I don't know what the world is coming to.

(ERIC *and* HECTOR *come, furtively, down the stairs. There are muffled warning sounds from* MARY.)

CASSIE: What is wrong with you, woman?

HECTOR: Just shut up and relax, Lady ...

(CASSIE *screams.*)

... and nothing will happen to you.

ERIC: Don't nothin' happen to you ... if you don't do nothin' crazy ...

HECTOR: Get somethin' and tie her up, man.

(*LIGHTS*)

(*Minutes later. The two boys are tying* CASSIE *to a chair.* MARY's *muffled weeping can be heard.*)

ERIC: I told you, man. I told you ...

CASSIE: My God ...

ERIC: ... she'd double back. I knew it! I knew it! "No!", he say, "She ain't doublin' back!" "How you know?!", I say. "I just know!", he say.

HECTOR: Shut up! I gotta think.

CASSIE: ... They're just babies.

ERIC: Great! Now ... he gonna think.

CASSIE: Y'all's just babies. Don't do this.

ERIC: Now ... we got this ol' lady to deal with ... he gonna think.

CASSIE: Please, don't do this.

ERIC: Now ... we got two ol' ladies to deal with ... he gonna think. Man, I knew we shouldn'ta come.

HECTOR: You know so damn much, why the hell you come . . .?

ERIC: 'Cause you say couldn't nothin' go wrong. "Trust me! Trust me!", he say. Shit . . . (*To* CASSIE) 'scuse me, Ma'am . . . You know so much. Well, how come you ain't know nothin' 'bout this other one?

HECTOR: You 'spect me to know everything?

ERIC: That's what you always sayin'. And she white, too?

(MARY *starts moving her head violently.*)

CASSIE: Take that thing from 'round her mouth. Can't you see the woman can't breathe. What's wrong with you?

(CASSIE's *tone startles* ERIC *into action and he removes* MARY's *gag, almost before he knows what he's doing.*)

HECTOR: What you do that for?

ERIC: She was chokin', man . . .

HECTOR: So? If she do, that's one we don't have to worry 'bout.

(MARY *catches her breath.*)

MARY: Don't come near me. Stay away!

ERIC: That's what I got in mind, lady.

HECTOR: See there . . .?

ERIC: Believe you me. Last thing I wanna do is come near you. Man, a white lady is a bad sign. My mom's always sayin' that and it's true.

HECTOR: Just find some more stuff to tie this one's feet.

ERIC: Should be gettin' the hell outta here.

CASSIE: You go easy there. That hurts!

HECTOR: Damn right! You ain't goin' nowhere . . .

ERIC: Ease up, man. You ain't got to be so rough.

HECTOR: How come?

ERIC: She old.

HECTOR: If I tie the other one up tight, it's okay with you?

ERIC: I don't give a kitty what you do with that one.

HECTOR: See, man. You prejudice. You want me to make nice with this one 'cause she black . . . like you . . .

ERIC: Just go easy . . . That's all.

HECTOR: Man, I turn her loose and soon as we turn our back, she be on the phone to the man . . .

CASSIE: What man?

ERIC: The cops . . .

MARY: There's no phone here.

CASSIE: Shut up, woman!

ERIC: Yeah! There ain't no phone, so they can't call nobody.

CASSIE: Listen to him, son . . .

HECTOR: Don't call me no "son". I ain't no "son" of your'n.

CASSIE: Y'all're both just babies to me . . .

HECTOR: I ain't no baby!

CASSIE: . . . .and y'all gonna mess up y'all's life forever if y'all do this.

HECTOR: Shut up!

ERIC: Ease up, man. You ain't got to yell at her. Let's just get the hell outta here.

HECTOR: No!

ERIC: Come on, Hector . . .

HECTOR: No! I ain't goin' nowhere 'till I get what I come for . . .

CASSIE: And what is that?

HECTOR: Money! Jewels! Diamonds! Gold! Shit!

CASSIE: Well, there's plenty of that last thing you mentioned, but ain't nothing like all the rest you say. What make y'all think I got stuff like that here?

HECTOR: Cut the crap, lady. Everybody know you got all kinds of money. 'Sides, now that I know this ain't even your house . . .

CASSIE: What?

HECTOR: . . . and you only work for this woman, here . . .

CASSIE: What you say?

HECTOR: . . . . I don't even have to talk to you. (*To* MARY) Where you keep the stuff, lady?

MARY: I don't know what . . .

CASSIE: This is my house, boy!

HECTOR: Say what?

CASSIE: She only live here. This is my house. Free and clear! Think 'cause I'm colored, I can't own nothin? This is my house.

HECTOR: Okay, then, you tell me where the stuff is . . .

CASSIE: Ain't no stuff here like what you lookin' for. I don't give a damn 'bout what "everybody" say 'bout me. Ain't nothin' like that stuff here. Ain't nothin' but bad memories in this house and you welcome to them, if you want 'em. Got some damn nerve. This is my house!

HECTOR: Suit yourself. We find it.

MARY: What are they going to do, Cassie?

CASSIE/HECTOR:

What you think they gonna do, woman?	What you think we gonna do, lady?

MARY: Don't let them hurt me, Cassie. You can't let them hurt me.

ERIC: Aw, shut up! Ain't nobody even studyin' you.

MARY: You promised you'd take care of me. You promised Daddy.

CASSIE: Ain't I been doing that? Hush up, now!

MARY: But I'm afraid.

CASSIE: Of what, Mary? What're you afraid of? Now listen, children.

HECTOR: Don't be callin . . .

CASSIE: I'm sorry, child, but that's what you are to me. I'm beggin' y'all to go. Untie me and go.

HECTOR: Lady, you know we can't go. You know what gonna happen.

ERIC: Ain't nothin' gonna happen . . .

CASSIE: Oh, I know you got that little gun . . .

HECTOR: Ain't afraid to use it, neither . . .

ERIC: Hey, man . . .

CASSIE: Nobody sayin' you are. The point is, I ain't afraid to die. I been livin' close to death too long to be scared by him now. I mean, if I had my 'druthers, I'd just as soon go in my sleep. Never did like pain. Had enough of it in my life. Ain't I, Mary?

MARY: You can't let them hurt me.

CASSIE: . . . but even pain stop . . . in time. The real point is, I couldn't rest easy knowin' you two little children did this. Y'all will have this . . . this mark on you for the rest of your life. Y'all so young. The world is in front of you . . .

HECTOR: I'm gonna . . . I gotta stuff something in her mouth . . .

CASSIE/ERIC: No!

HECTOR: Then . . . tell her to shut up.

CASSIE: (*To* ERIC) Don't worry, son. I ain't sayin' nothin' more to him . . .

HECTOR: That's better . . .

CASSIE: . . . he's gone . . . already!

HECTOR: Okay, Eric. Square business. If you wanna go, go! I'm stayin'. Now that we got 'em tied up and quiet, I ain't see nothin' to change my plans. Well, you stayin'?

(ERIC *nods*.)

HECTOR: Okay! I'm goin' back upstairs . . . finish checkin' out them rooms. Keep your eye on'em!

ERIC: They can't do nothin', man. They just two frail, old ladies.

HECTOR: What's "frail"?

ERIC: Hah! So you don't know everything?

HECTOR: I'm goin' upstairs, clown . . .

(HECTOR *goes*.)

ERIC: (*Calling after him*) "Frail" mean old. That's what it mean. Heard my moms call my grandma that . . .

HECTOR: (*From the stairs*) I knew that, man.

MARY: I want to go to my room. I don't want to be here. Cassie, tell this boy to take me to my room . . .

ERIC: "Boy" hang out with Tarzan.

MARY: . . . and then you come and join me. I don't want to be here. Tell him . . .

CASSIE: Tell him yourself . . .

MARY: No, Cassie. I can't talk to him . . .

ERIC: Hey! Where you get off givin' orders? You all tied up and givin' orders. Who you think you are . . .?

MARY: Don't come near me! Don't you touch me?

CASSIE: This can't be little, sweet Miss Mary Majeski. Can't be cute, little Miss Mary Majeski sayin' she don't want a colored man's hands on her. Well, you sure have changed, Miss Mary Majeski. Time was when you couldn't get enough . . .

ERIC: What you talkin' 'bout, lady?

CASSIE: Oh, nothin', son. Just the past. If you was older . . . If you wasn't such a cute, little thing, you'd see that all this is just the past. Don't concern you . . . and it shouldn't. You should be thinkin' 'bout your future . . . and not our past.

ERIC: You sound like my grandma.

CASSIE: Your "frail", old grandma? She old like me, son?

ERIC: Guess so. My moms don't like puttin' up with her.

CASSIE: Oh?

ERIC: She ain't so bad. She okay with me.

CASSIE: Well, she won't have too much longer to live. She be out her misery soon.

ERIC: What you mean, lady?

CASSIE: When she find out what you doin', it gonna kill her . . .

ERIC: No!

CASSIE: Yes. It gonna kill her outright. I know grandmas and I bet yours is some crazy 'bout you . . .

ERIC: Okay, lady. I think you oughtta shut up . . . I mean . . . I don't think you oughtta say no more to me . . .

CASSIE: . . . and I know she always telling you to be good and learn . . .

MARY: Don't talk to him, Cassie.

CASSIE: . . . Always tryin' to tell you the difference 'tween right and wrong.

ERIC: Come on, lady.

CASSIE: . . . 'cause she want you to 'mount to something . . .

ERIC: Yeah . . . but . . .

CASSIE: . . . just like I told you to think of your future . . .

MARY: I don't want you to talk to him.

CASSIE: . . . That's why I remind you of your sweet, ol' grandma . . . who loves you . . . and Mary . . . if you don't shut up . . .

HECTOR: (*From upstairs*) Hey, man. Come up here. There's some strange doors up here.

CASSIE: How come you followin' after that one . . . ?

ERIC: I ain't followin' after him . . .

CASSIE: The way it look to me . . .

ERIC: Well, I ain't. I don't follow after nobody. I do what I like.

CASSIE: Oh, I see . . .

ERIC: He my man! He my homeboy!

CASSIE: He ain't no homeboy of your'n.

ERIC: You don't get it. We just together. I help him. He help me.

CASSIE: But, he leadin' you! He takin' everything from you. He talk like you. He walk like you. He leadin' you and stealing everything 'bout you. You can't see that? He think he white and . . .

ERIC: No he ain't . . .

CASSIE: I didn't say he was. I said he think he is. He think he as white as this one here . . . and they always try to steal everything we got. I ain't kiddin'. He talk colored. He act colored. If I was to close my eyes, I'd swear he was colored. If your skin'd do him some good, he'd take that and wear it. That's the way they operate.

ERIC: He ain't white, ma'am.

CASSIE: Try tellin' him that.

ERIC: He Spanish.

CASSIE: They all think they white. When y'all get caught, he gonna be white and he gonna go free. You goin' straight to the 'lectric chair. . . .

ERIC: 'Lectric chair? See . . . you tryin' to scare me but you just comin' off funny.

CASSIE: Then, I'm sorry, son. I wish I could scare you into not doin' this.

ERIC: Ma'am, Hector an me together 'cause one day some guys was messin' me over on the "el". He ain't say nothin'. I ain't even know him. All I know is, there's somebody else hittin' them cats 'sides me. He just start in swingin'. Well, we ain't 'xactly win the duke, but we ain't lose neither. Them guys stop jackin' us up, though. We tight ever since. He ain't gonna turn on me. And I ain't goin' to no 'lectric chair. They can't do nothin' to me. I ain't old enough . . .

HECTOR: Ain't you hear me, man?

ERIC: Keep your shirt on. I'm comin'. (*To* CASSIE) See, I'm what they call a "juvenile offender".

CASSIE: You a black "juvenile offender".

ERIC: I'm too young to even get my name in the papers.

(*Calling to* HECTOR *as he goes off laughing.*)

What you want, man?

HECTOR: (*From upstairs*) There's two big doors up here. I can't get 'em open.

ERIC: "With these keys, I can open any door in Chicago." Ain't that what you said?

HECTOR: Just come on up and help me, man.

CASSIE: They'll just shoot you, son. Just shoot you and get rid of you . . . once and for all. You ain't even important. They'll just shoot you. That's what they always do. They get rid of our men . . . one way or the other. Lord! Lord! Lord!

(*The deep, throaty laughter of* AARON *is heard again, mingled this time with that of the young* MARY.)

MARY: Oh, my God! My dear, sweet, wonderful and beautiful God!

AARON: That was good, Ma'am.

MARY: No! Don't say anything! Not a word! Don't spoil the moment. At least . . . don't spoil it with . . . "That was good, Ma'am . . ."

AARON: What you want me to say, Ma'am.

MARY: If you want to say something, tell me about the moon. Tell me about the stars. Tell me that there's never been a Goddess like me. Tell me I'm a beautiful, white queen, but if all that you have to say is, "That was good", then don't say anything. Don't move a muscle 'till I say so!

AARON: Ma'am . . .

MARY: Ssshh! Ssshh! Not a word!

AARON: I gotta go.

MARY: Oh, damn it. You're ruining the moment.

AARON: It's time to go pick up Cassie.

MARY: Well, damn it, if you're so worried about her, get out. Just get the hell out of here. What can she do? Have me put in jail for corrupting your morals? What can she do? Is she white? I could have you both thrown in jail, if I wanted to. Don't you worry your wooly head about what she'll do. Worry about me. Suppose I tell my father that you just came in here and took advantage of me.

(*The light comes up behind the portrait.*)

AARON: He'd believe you, Ma'am.

MARY: I'd do it, you know. I could do it.

AARON: I know you could, Ma'am.

MARY: I lower myself and he wants to go. I completely debase myself for this ape and he comes up with, "That was good."

AARON: Ma'am, I said that was good because that's just what it was. Good . . . but it wasn't Heaven. I'm sorry, but that's Cassie. Cassie is Heaven.

MARY: If she's so much Heaven, how come . . .

AARON: 'Cause I'm Earth, Ma'am. Cassie always was much better than I could be. I'm Earth, Ma'am . . . and so are you. We just sort of dirt . . . together . . . Ma'am.

MARY: How dare you. All I have to do is run to the window and scream and you're as good as dead . . .

AARON: Guess you could do that, Ma'am. Lord knows if you did, everybody'd believe you, wouldn't they? I'd run. They'd probably catch me. So, might as well make it worth the while . . .

MARY: What're you going to do?

AARON: Nothin' you don't want done, Ma'am. . . .

MARY: Oh, God! You're . . . you're . . . wonderful.

AARON: Your servant, Ma'am.

(*Lights down. Then, a beat later, lights up.*)

MARY: You know I was only teasing you. You know me and my silly little jokes. Cassie can't be back for another hour. Stay. Stay. Please? See what you make me do? See how you make me beg you? Cassie never has to beg you, does she? That's what you like, isn't it? You like seeing a white woman beg, don't you? I've never done it before . . . to anyone. Especially to a big, black prince. That's what you are, you know. My big, black jungle prince. My Kong of Kongs. I'm your slave, now. We could leave here. You could take me anywhere. I'd do things for you Cassie never dreamed of . . .

AARON: Doubt that, Ma'am. Cassie done things with me I ain't never dreamed of.

MARY: Bastard!

AARON: . . . You ain't gonna like hearing this, Ma'am . . . but I'm used to it . . . the white ladies . . that is. Ain't nothin' new or unusual 'bout it . . .

MARY: Bastard!

AARON: . . . but you did say you wanted to hear 'bout the moon . . . You did say you wanted some talk 'bout the stars. Well, I been there. Every night I'm with Cassie, I go past 'em to wherever.

MARY: Bastard!

AARON: . . . That's why I mess 'round every once in a blue moon. Cassie too much for a ordinary sport like myself. Every night . . . Heaven! Every night . . . Paradise! It's enough to kill a man, Ma'am . . . but leave Cassie? Why, I'd be a goddamned fool!

MARY: Bastard!

AARON: Your servant, Ma'am!

(*They laugh together.* AARON *disappears gradually. The lights go down on* MARY *and come up full on the portrait.*)

MAJESKI: Maria! You are abomination. You break the heart of your father. Like your mother, you are. Like your mother, you kill my heart. Better I never come to this place . . . this America. I try to be American and marry American girl. I try to be good American. I try to be what I am not. I try to be good husband. I try to be good father. Everything crumbles. Everything goes. I do everything for you . . . after you mother run off. Everything is for you when I die. All is for you. I hear everybody laughing at me and I take it all . . . all for you, Maria. Now there is no you. Now, there is no Maria. Is only a daughter who break the heart of a father. Better, I never come to this place . . . this America.

(*The light comes up on the young-voiced* CASSIE.)

CASSIE: So you just gonna sit here and be broken-hearted and die? Well, you sit there, be broken hearted and die by yourself. I ain't mopin' with you. I'm leavin'.

MAJESKI: You leave?

CASSIE: I don't chew my cabbage twice.

MAJESKI: Where do you go?

CASSIE: 'Way from here!

MAJESKI: You go to find them?

CASSIE: Them?

MAJESKI: Him?

CASSIE: What for? He ain't worth lookin' for and I don't know what I'd do if I caught 'em. Probably kill that daughter of your'n.

MAJESKI: I have no daughter! My daughter is dead!

CASSIE: Don't talk like a fool.

MAJESKI: I have no daughter!

CASSIE: Yes, you do . . . damn it . . . and she off somewhere with my man 'cause you tell him to get out! You the one send my man off!

MAJESKI: I am the one who see them together.

CASSIE: It woulda pass. It's just a little sickness colored men go through when they get a whiff of pink tuna . . . but it passes. You hear? It woulda pass.

MAJESKI: I see them in her room. I hear the things she say to him. The things he make her say. I see the things she do to him. The things he make her do. I cannot speak. I have no voice. I cannot move. I cannot even move to kill them. He make me not move. I have to stand there . . . and watch. I cannot move. He make me not move.

CASSIE: You make him sound like a conjure man or somthin'. She the one make him do them things. She a witch! A white witch! She wave all that red hair in front his body. She wear all that perfume and let him see all her white skin.

MAJESKI: He put spell on her . . .

CASSIE: . . . Your daughter the witch . . .

MAJESKI: He is evil . . .

CASSIE: . . . a evil witch!

MAJESKI: He put spell on her. Make her do evil things.

CASSIE: She throw all that white skin at him.

MAJESKI: Evil . . .

CASSIE: Evil!

MAJESKI: . . . Evil, black nigger!

CASSIE: Now, you hold on! It's all right for me to call him that . . . but you . . you watch your damn mouth. Don't you call him no "nigger".

How you even wrap your lips to form such a word. Think you American or something, don't you? Y'all foreigners come over here and call anybody any damn thing y'all want to, don't you? Don't you be usin' that word again or I'll poison your foreign ass. Can't talk English good, but I'll bet "nigger" was the first word y'all learn when you come off the boat. Just 'cause some "nigger" . . . that's right . . . I can say it . . not you . . . 'cause some nigger been in bed with your treasure, you go crazy and say things like it ain't happen before and ain't gonna happen again. Yeah, they probably together right now. Right this minute . . laughing at you . . . and me! Dammit! And you know what? When you die, she gonna come back here like nothin' ever happen and spend all your money . . . probably on him . . .

MAJESKI: No!

CASSIE: Probably sell this house and give him all the money . . .

MAJESKI: No!

CASSIE: Sure as daylight comin' tomorrow.

MAJESKI: No! I burn down this house first. I burn the money!

CASSIE: Don't talk like a damn ass. Don't be no fool, fool! That ain't gettin' back at him . . .

MAJESKI: I don't care about him!

CASSIE: Well, you oughtta. Who you think gonna be livin' with her? Spendin' your money? The money you work so hard for. If it ain't him, it's gonna be some other "nigger". The girl got black fever. Don't that just rile you? Sure it do? You know how you hate that. You know how that just go against your foreign grain. No, you can't do nothin' stupid. You gotta get back at 'em! Both of them!

MAJESKI: How?

CASSIE: Wonder what they doing . . . right now. You think they makin' time right this very minute.

MAJESKI: You stop!

CASSIE: You think, that even while we here talkin', he got his thick, long, black . . .

MAJESKI: You stop!

CASSIE: . . .arms . . . 'round your little pink daughter?

MAJESKI: Stop

CASSIE: Think he could be kissin' her all over with them lips of his? I know them lips, you know. Make a woman do anything. Think that's goin' on?

MAJESKI: No! No!

CASSIE: . . . or maybe, he and her doin' . . . you know . . . Oh, he real good at that. Think they makin' "pakootcheepap" . . . right now?

MAJESKI: You shut up you filthy mouth . . .

CASSIE: . . . or maybe . . . by now . . he done put you a little half-black grandchild in your lily-white princess . . .

MAJESKI: No! No!

CASSIE: . . . or maybe . . . by now . . she done made him mad and he slappin' her 'round a bit. Just slappin' your daughter . . .

MAJESKI: No!

CASSIE: . . . and her carrying your half-black grandchild . . . too. She probably like that.

MAJESKI: You go. Go or I throw you out!

CASSIE: Yeah . . . Be just like her to love being hit by that big, black . . .

MAJESKI: Stop! Please, stop! It is a sight I cannot bear to think on. If she were standing before me, this minute, I would kill her. I would put my hands around her throat and choke away the life I gave her. I would choke out all her sins and never let them come out for the world to breathe. I should have kill her when I see them together. I should have kill her . . .

CASSIE: And she would laugh at you from Hell. You want to do something to make her feel your pain?

MAJESKI: She should have pain!

CASSIE: Want to do something to hurt her?

MAJESKI: I want her to feel how she hurt me!

CASSIE: Want to do something to punish her?

MAJESKI: I want to punish her for what she do to me . . . and to God!

CASSIE: You want to punish her for being such an ungrateful daughter . . . and takin' my man?

MAJESKI: Yes! Yes! I hate her!

CASSIE: Want to do something that will make it impossible for her to get her hands on your money and your house and your business so she can give it to him or whatever other . . . "nigger" . . . she choose . . .?

MAJESKI: Yes! Yes! Tell me what to do!

CASSIE: Marry me!

MAJESKI: What you are saying . . . ?

CASSIE: You heard me.

MAJESKI: You are crazy woman . . .

CASSIE: Don't even think it!

MAJESKI: You . . . are . . . crazy . . .

CASSIE: Who you got left in this world, old man? How much longer you got left, old man? Marry me and she'll never get her hands on your money . . . or this house . . or our business . . . or anything else of mine again . . .

MAJESKI: Is ridiculous! The people in this neighborhood . . . they would never let you live here. They don't want your kind here.

CASSIE: They let you live here and they don't want your kind, either . . .

MAJESKI: I am white!

CASSIE: . . . and you foreign . . .

MAJESKI: But I am white!

CASSIE: . . . and I'm your colored maid. I'm livin' here now, ain't I?

MAJESKI: Because you are the maid.

CASSIE: So? Who gonna tell'em different? I ain't and neither are you. Only two people in this world have to know. Justice of the Peace . . . and . . . your lawyer. Our lawyer!

MAJESKI: You would go this far?

CASSIE: Question is, would you?

MAJESKI: You are different woman. You are hard woman. I always think of you as . . .

CASSIE: . . . just a maid. A slave . . . pickin' up after you. Cleanin' your mess. Cleanin' up after you and your messy, spoiled princess . . .

MAJESKI: . . . but you are hard woman . . . with hard heart . . .

CASSIE: You don't know nothin' 'bout my heart. I might not even have one. You gonna do it . . . or not?

MAJESKI: You must promise me . . .

CASSIE: What?

MAJESKI: When is all over and he leave her, you find her and bring her back here to stay. I fix it all up with lawyer. I fix you too, Cassie, *and* I fix her. If anything happen to her ... if she die too quick ... you give all up ... all money go to the Church. If anything happen to you and is not natural cause ... she get nothing ... I tell lawyer to fix ... and you take care of my little girl. She must not die quick. She must suffer ... yes ... you take care of my little Maria ... you do that?

CASSIE: I do that!

MAJESKI: We play big joke on her, eh, Cassie?

CASSIE: Big joke. Oh, by the way ... if we gonna be man and wife ... how you pronounce your first name ...?

(CASSIE's *laughter joins that of* MAJESKI. *The laughter amplifies. The lights go out and, after a few short beats, come up again ... as before, on the laughing portrait and* CASSIE.)

MAJESKI: So ... now you are the first colored Mrs. Wladek Majeski ...

CASSIE: And, now ... you don't have to be bumpin' into me or rubbin' up against me on the sly. Now, you don't have to be lookin' at me and wishin' you was with me instead of standin' outside me and Aaron's door ... listenin'. Oh, I know you. Your daughter ... our daughter caught the black fever from you.

MAJESKI: You are laughing at me?

CASSIE: Hell, no! Just want to let you know I'm gonna live up to my end. You gonna get what you paid for. You can die happy because all this belong to you now.

MAJESKI: You will not laugh at me?

CASSIE: Tonight, I'm gonna lay some stuff on you gonna take you to the moon and back and you can die happy. In fact, Mr. Majeski, now you can die just any old time you want to ...

(*The eerie lights go out and immediately the main light comes up full.*)

HECTOR: Hey, Lady, how you get them doors open?

CASSIE: What?

HECTOR: Them two funny doors with them things on it won't open. Them's got to be the rooms where you keep all the treasure, ain't it? How you open 'em?

MARY: My room? Is he talking about my old room? My room and Daddy's room had special doors. You won't let them go in my old room, will you Cassie?

CASSIE: ... and how am I supposed to stop him, my darling daughter?

ERIC: Them doors even look special. All them funny-lookin' statues and stuff on 'em . . .

HECTOR: Them's carvin's . . .

ERIC: Look like the kind of whittlin' my grandpa used to do.

HECTOR: That's how I know they special.

CASSIE: You right. There used to be mighty precious treasure in one of them rooms . . . but it's down here now.

HECTOR: I don't know what you talkin' 'bout. Just tell me how I get in them rooms.

CASSIE: You really want to look?

MARY: No! No! There's nothing in my room. Only a lot of dead memories. Old secrets that should never come out. Old wounds that should not bleed again. The past keeps that door locked. It's sealed with the nails of memory.

HECTOR: That's it! I know there's shit in there now. When they start talking crazy like that . . . there's got to be a whole lotta good stuff in there . . .

MARY: Don't let them defile my room.

CASSIE: Would you like the keys?

ERIC AND HECTOR: Yeah!

MARY: No! There are ghosts up there . . .

HECTOR: Oh, shit . . .

MARY: . . . ghosts that will not sleep. Ghosts that have been waiting to be free.

CASSIE: She don't know what she talkin' bout. See that urn over there?

ERIC: Urn?

HECTOR: Ghosts . .?

MARY: . . . Terrible spirits who should stay locked up there . . .

HECTOR: Maybe . . . we oughtta just look through the stuff in the drawers down here . . .

CASSIE: Yes . . . that urn! That vase! That . . . jar. There!

ERIC: This thing?

CASSIE: Yes. Bring it here. It holds the ashes of my dead husband.

ERIC AND HECTOR: What?

MARY: Oh, my God! You never told me . . .

CASSIE: He locked a door and told me it was never to be opened. He carried the key for the little, short time we was married. So when he went, I put the key in with him. Sealed him and the key to his precious treasure room shut!

MARY: You never told me . . .

CASSIE: You want the key, take it! You want the key to the other room take it. It's 'round my neck. Come on, son. I want you to take it.

ERIC: Okay. I ain't scared . .

HECTOR: Man, don't be foolin' 'round with no dead people ashes . . .

CASSIE: Take it, son. Take the key. Who cares now?

(ERIC *takes the key from* CASSIE'S *neck.*)

MARY: You never told me . . .

ERIC: How I get the other one out?

HECTOR: Hey, man . . .

CASSIE: I said it was sealed. Even a big time "juvenile offender" like you oughtta be able to figure out that there's only one way to get the key out . . .

(*After some pondering,* ERIC *smashes the urn to the floor.* MARY *screams.* HECTOR *crosses himself as* ERIC *picks the key from the ashes.*)

HECTOR: Madre de Diós!

MARY: Ojciec! Ojciec! Ojciec!

CASSIE: Now, you go up to the doors and just lift up the carved face that's right in the middle and the lock's right under there.

ERIC: You ain't lyin' now . . . ?

CASSIE: Go on up and see!

ERIC: You comin' . . . or you scared?

HECTOR: Okay, Eric.

(*They go off,* HECTOR *following* ERIC. *The lights soften . . . on young-voiced* CASSIE *and* MARY.)

CASSIE: So, he left you, hunh? Left you high and dry! Look at you. Can you move at all? Doctor say I can take you home in a week or so. Why don't you say something? Cat got your tongue?

MARY: I want my father!

CASSIE: What happened? Why'd he beat you? Why'd he get tired of you? Did he keep seeing my face? Never mind! We won't even speak 'bout him no more. You try and get some rest. You just try. Just rest and think 'bout how Cassie gonna take care of you for as long as you live. Cassie gonna take you home to her big house 'cause she know you gonna be ever so comfortable there. Too bad you can't have your old room back . . . but your father sealed it up . . . and he got the key with him. Say it remind him of too many things. Anyway, it's too big for you and besides . . . now you can't get 'round so good. But don't you worry. I got a nice little room fixed up for you downstairs. Used to be me and Aaron's room. You remember? You'll be happy there. Well, I guess I better get going. Got to make arrangements to get my little, white stepdaughter home to my house where I can take good care of her and pay her back for all the kindness she done me. Oh, by the way . . . your father died!

(*Lights fade and in the darkness . . .*)

MARY: Ojciec! Ojciec! Ojciec!

(*Lights come up full.*)

MARY: Cassie?

CASSIE: Yes, Mary.

MARY: Are they going to kill us?

CASSIE: Could be.

MARY: I don't want it to hurt.

CASSIE: You think I do?

MARY: They're going to kill us. . . . These two children are going to end our lives . . .

CASSIE: They so young and stupid and scared, ain't no tellin' what they'll do.

MARY: Maybe. . . . Maybe its time we died.

CASSIE: Maybe so. Maybe we both should've been dead long ago, but nobody's got the right to kill us. If I can't kill you or you can't kill me . . . nobody else got the right.

MARY: There's something I want you to know . . .

CASSIE: Well, I guess I'm gonna sure 'nough die, now. Always figured that on the day my time come, I'd hear you sayin', "There's something I want you to know. . . ." Well, let's have it.

MARY: He loved you. Aaron loved you.

CASSIE: I know that.

AARON'S VOICE: I never stopped lovin' you, Cassie.

MARY: But you never told him you loved him. You never said those words.

CASSIE: I thought he knew.

MARY: That's why he would beat me. He loved you.

AARON'S VOICE: At first . . . I didn't know what to do without you . . .

(MARY's *voice will alternate between young and old as is appropriate to the next exchange.* AARON *will gradually appear.*)

MARY: He had no life to him. "Why don't you go back to your precious Cassie, if you're so dead::" He slapped me.

AARON: Don't you call her name!

MARY: He slapped me and said . . .

AARON: You ain't good enough to call her name. Don't call her name.

MARY: . . . just kept slapping me and in his rage, he'd take me. . . . Calling your name and saying how you never told him you loved him. You never said the words . . .

CASSIE: I thought he knew.

MARY: He wanted to hear the words . . .

CASSIE: He didn't know me. I never was one to shout my pleasures. I thought it was enough just givin' him pleasure. He shoulda known that. It's the way I am.

AARON: Cassie! Cassie! Cassie!

MARY: . . . With every movement. Doing me and slapping me. Oh, God, how he hurt . . .

AARON: Love that, don't you. You make me hit you 'cause you just crazy 'bout it . . .

MARY: Whenever those times hit him, I had only to mention your name and he'd become this wild, stormy thing. Whiskey didn't do it. Most times we'd kick the gong around . . . but . . .

AARON: . . . reefer couldn't do it . . .

MARY: . . . only my mentioning your name would do it. He'd come to life and hit me. He'd tell me . . .

AARON: You made me dirty. I ain't fit for Cassie. Ain't fit for nobody, now, 'cept you . . .

MARY: . . . then, he'd take me, Cassie. I always wondered how you felt when the two of you were together. I'd listen outside your room . . . sometimes. I'd hear him groaning . . . but I never heard you. I wanted to be in there groaning with him. I wanted to make him groan and growl like I heard him doing with you. I wondered if you felt like I felt . . . but I never heard you. The last time, I guess it was too much. We'd come east. My money was runnin' out . . .

". . . and you got me in this filthy place . . ."

AARON: You lucky we got this place. Ain't too many places in Harlem willin' to take me . . . long as I got you along . . .

MARY: You hit me and I go straight to the police and tell 'em you kidnapped me.

AARON: That shit mighta work before . . . but you in my territory now.

MARY: It had always worked before. He'd always get scared when I told him that and he'd calm down.

". . . I'll scream my head off . . ."

AARON: Go 'head . . .

MARY: Even in Harlem the police don't want you hittin' no white woman.

AARON: Let 'em come. I don't give a good goddamn. Let 'em come and tell 'em I killed your evil, white ass in the bargain . . .

MARY: That was it. He just started in on me. Just kept hittin' me over and over again . . . and each time . . . he screamed . . .

AARON: Cassie! Cassie! Cassie!

(As AARON screams, so do the two boys from upstairs.)

MARY: I just couldn't take it anymore . . .

(ERIC and HECTOR come running down.)

ERIC: One of the rooms . . . one of the rooms . . . it got a coffin in it . . .

CASSIE: I told you what you'd be lookin' for wasn't up there . . .

HECTOR: Let's get the hell outta here. I wanna go. Let's go. You hear, let's go!

ERIC: You don't want to look around no more?

HECTOR: No!

ERIC: I think we oughta look 'round some more . . .

HECTOR: Let's go! Please?

ERIC: Little while ago . . . you was hot to stay . . .

HECTOR: Little while ago . . . you was hot to go. What change your mind . . .?

ERIC: I don't appreciate nobody tryin' to scare the shit outta me like that. You hear that, lady. Now, I ain't foolin' 'round no more. We come here for money, ain't we? That's what you said, ain't you? Well . . . let's get some. Hey, lady . . . yeah, you! Any money in this damn house . . . and don't lie or it gonna be your last. I ain't jivin' no more. I'm serious . . .

HECTOR: Hey . . . what's wrong with you, Bro?

ERIC: Don't be callin' me that. I said you got any money . . .?

MARY: Yes! Yes, I have money. I'll show you. I'll show you.

HECTOR: What I tell you?

ERIC: Yeah, yeah! You told me. No, Lady. You tell me where it is and I go get it.

MARY: It's just a little box. You untie me and take me to my room . . . and I'll open it . . .

ERIC: No untyin' . . .

CASSIE: She don't know what she talkin' 'bout.

HECTOR: Hell, I'll untie her. Money's what we come for.

ERIC: I said, "No!" Now, where is this box?

MARY: In my room . . . under my pillow . . .

CASSIE: What you talkin' 'bout, Mary?

ERIC: I go get it. Watch 'em!

(ERIC goes.)

MARY: It's just a little Chinese puzzle box . . .

HECTOR: Who he think he is?

MARY: It belongs to you . . .

(HECTOR starts to untie MARY.)

CASSIE: What you doing, boy?

MARY: Aaron bought it for you . . .

HECTOR: . . . givin' me orders like I'm some slave . . .

MARY: He got it for you . . . years ago . . .

HECTOR: Tellin' me what to do . . .

MARY: He put money in it and had to trust me to send it . . .

HECTOR: . . . and don't you think 'bout tryin' nothin' . . .

MARY: . . . because he couldn't even write his name . . .

HECTOR: . . . I still got this . . . you know . . .

MARY: . . . but he wanted you to have it . .

CASSIE: All this time.

HECTOR: Now . . . you, Lady . . .

(HECTOR *starts to untie* CASSIE.)

MARY: He should have loved me . . .

HECTOR: . . . and don't you try nothin' neither . . .

MARY: He should have loved me the way I loved him . . .

CASSIE: . . . Just untie me, Boy!

HECTOR: . . . Ain't no "boy" . . . dammit!

CASSIE: Okay, Mister. Just untie me!

(ERIC *comes out with the box.*)

ERIC: Here 'tis. Tell me how to open it . . . or I bust it all to shit . . .

(ERIC *notices that* MARY *is free and* HECTOR *is about to free* CASSIE.)

ERIC: Hey! What you think you doin', Man?

HECTOR: What it look like I'm doin?

CASSIE: Untie me, son!

MARY: Give me the box . . .

ERIC: Didn't I say, "No untyin'"?

CASSIE: It don't belong to you . .

HECTOR: That's why I'm doin' it. Don't nobody tell me what to do . . .

CASSIE: It's mine.

ERIC: Oh, no?

HECTOR: No! You don't like it?

ERIC: No!

HECTOR: Well, why'nt you try and do somethin' 'bout it? (*He brandishes his gun.*) Yeah. Figured this bad boy'd pull you up short. Don't wanna break so bad and give orders with big Roscoe starin' you in the face . . . do you, Nigger?

(ERIC, *infuriated, tackles* HECTOR. *The gun falls to the floor.* MARY *rises from the wheel chair and with box, gets behind* CASSIE, *who is wide-eyed with disbelief.*)

CASSIE: You evil witch! You evil, white witch!

(ERIC *and* HECTOR *continue scrapping on the floor.*)

CASSIE: All these years. Waitin' on you . . . hand and foot. Fixin' your food. Emptyin' your pan. Cleanin' your mess. Doin' for you. Keepin' your behin' alive. All these years and you . . . you can walk? Ain't enough you had to have my man. Ain't enough you had to have Aaron. You had to have my life, too? You evil, white witch. Stop it! Stop it, you two worthless pieces of shit. Stop it and get up from there! Quit that scuffin' and kill her! Kill her! Stop it, I say! Stop it and kill her. Shoot her! Take your gun and shoot her!

(MARY, *transfixed, walks over and picks up the gun.*)

Don't let her get the gun . . .

(*Not really knowing what to do with the gun,* MARY *regards it curiously, turning it over in her hands.*)

You fools! I told you to kill her. I told you to shoot her rotten, worthless, lyin', evil, stealin' ass.

(CASSIE *dissolves into tears, but her last bit of tirade pricks* MARY *into momentary reality. She aims at the two boys and emits a galvanizing scream.*)

MARY: STOP IT! STOP IT!

(ERIC *and* HECTOR *freeze in terror, although* HECTOR's *is only fleeting and he, immediately, relaxes somewhat.*)

Get up from there.

CASSIE: (*Sobbing*) I hate you.

ERIC: Don't shoot! Please, Lady. I'll go and never come back . . Please, Lady, don't shoot me. I don't wanna die. (*He sobs in fear.*)

CASSIE: I hope your soul burns in Hell . . . forever

HECTOR: Shut up, man. Hey, Lady . . . you gonna shoot us? Go 'head. Shoot us if you wanna, Shoot us if you gonna. Hey, I made a poem. Aw, shit, man. Stop with the cryin'. She ain't gonna do nothin'. She can't. The damn gun don't work.

(HECTOR *starts to laugh.*)

HECTOR: The gun don't work, man.

ERIC: Bet?

HECTOR: Bet!

(MARY *is taken aback at this news.*)

Go 'head, Lady. Hit me with your best shot!

(HECTOR *offers his chest as a target.* MARY *squeezes the trigger, but aside from some clicks, nothing happens.* MARY, *dejectedly, lets the gun fall.* HECTOR *picks it up and turns on* ERIC.)

Ain't you feel shame? Blubberin' and shit. "Please, Lady, don't shoot me. I won't do it no more."

ERIC: Quit laughin' at me . . .

HECTOR: Can't help it. You was funny.

ERIC: Wish I had. . . . Wish I could find somethin'. A stick. . . . Somethin'. . . . Lady, if I had my baseball bat, I'd break your head open . . .

CASSIE: You're lost, son.

ERIC: You pull me down in front of my man. Don't nobody do that to me . . .

CASSIE: You like a young wolf tastin' blood for the first . . .

ERIC: I'm gonna find somethin' and kill the hell out of you. . . .

CASSIE: . . . Lost . . .

HECTOR: Man, let's just get the hell away from this crazy-ass house. We got enough stuff . . .

ERIC: Crazy-ass women! Spooky-ass house! Big, ol' coffin sittin' up there just like that. Oughta off'em just for the hell of it. Y'all better don't call no police neither or I be comin' back and . . .

HECTOR: They crazy, man. Who'd believe 'em. Even if they do call the man . . all you gotta do is look innocent and sweet and smile like you was lost and helpless. Look at us! Would you put these faces in the slams?

(*For a moment, their faces are frozen in their most innocent smiles.*)

ERIC: C'mon, my man.

HECTOR: I'm with you, Bro!

(*They go off and out, laughing and carrying their back-packs with their pitiful knick-knacks. As they get to the outer area, still laughing...*)

ERIC: Next time, man, I pick the job ...

HECTOR: Square business!

(*They exit.*)

MARY: We're safe, now. It's just the two of us again.

CASSIE: Untie me!

MARY: It won't be like before. I can help with things ...

CASSIE: Untie me!

MARY: I can take care of you. Won't that be nice, for a change?

CASSIE: You better untie me, woman!

MARY: Here's the box, Cassie. It's yours. There's something in there for you.

CASSIE: Mary ...?

MARY: Just a pitiable thing, but he meant for you to have it.

CASSIE: Untie me, Mary. Please.

MARY: Oh ... yes.

(MARY *undoes the rest of* CASSIE'S *bonds.*)

This is how it should be. Just you and me. Here! Alone!

CASSIE: Alone ...?

(CASSIE *starts to laugh.*)

Alone? No, Mary. We ain't alone. Ain't never been alone. Ain't never gonna be alone.

MARY: Cassie ...?

CASSIE: While you was in the hospital, I went and got him. I went and got the little bit of him you left. Why didn't you just kill him outright? Why'd you have to do it ... a little bit at a time?

MARY: 'Cause he was killing me ... a little bit at a time. Every time he called your name, he killed a little bit of me. That night, as he slept, I knew he'd call your name.

AARON: Cassie . . .

MARY: . . . As I heated the water, I knew he'd call your name . . .

AARON: Cassie . . .

MARY: . . . As it boiled . . . I knew he'd called your name . . .

AARON: Cassie . . .

MARY: . . . As I walked over to him, I knew he'd call your name . . .

AARON: Cassie.

MARY: As I poured the first pot all over his face . . . All in his eyes, I knew he'd call your name . . .

AARON: CASSIE . . .

MARY: . . . As I poured the second pot over him . . . letting the water spill slowly . . . all over his mesmerizing nethers . . .

AARON: CASSIE . . . CASSIE . . . CASSIE!!!

MARY: . . . And . . . finally . . .

AARON: CASSIE!!!

MARY: He should have loved me! I would have done it all for him. I would have dug rocks with my bare teeth . . . I would have wallowed in mud . . . I would have eaten fire . . . I would have blown up the whole world . . . I would have killed God for him. He should have loved me. Always . . . always . . . calling your name . . .

CASSIE: I brought him here to die . . .

MARY: . . . and you never told him you loved him . . .

CASSIE: He knew! He found out just how much! See, Mary, no matter how much you loved him, it wasn't enough. You only loved him enough to kill God, I loved him enough to kill him . . . and . . . to thank me . . . he died . . . calling my name.

AARON: Cassie . . .

MARY: He should have loved me . . .

CASSIE: He called my name every night. What I didn't tell him in life . . . I tell him now. You listen, Mary. You hear him callin' my name?

AARON: Cassie? Sweet Cassie? My Cassie?

CASSIE: You hear him, Mary? I'll be with him tonight. One way or the other, I'll be with him tonight. I'm with him every night . . . and every night . . . he calls my name.

AARON: My sweet Cassie!

MARY: He should have loved me!

CASSIE: And for that, we been here being mean to each other all this time. For that, you made me do things to you . . . all this time . . .

MARY: It was worth it . . . to see you suffer without him. He should have loved me. That big, black, beautiful nigger . . . should have loved me. Aaron, you should have loved me!

AARON: Always loved you, Cassie. Only you.

MARY: I won't listen. I won't hear! I just won't hear!

CASSIE: I know that . . .

MARY: I don't hear anything . . .

AARON: Forgive me. . . .

CASSIE: Long ago! You know that.

MARY AND CASSIE: It's just you and me here . . .

MARY: Cassie . . .

MARY AND CASSIE: . . . Just you and me. Nobody else is here. Nobody else matters. It's just you and me . . Just you and me . . .

CASSIE: . . . Aaron.

MARY AND CASSIE AND AARON: . . . Just like it should be . . .

AARON: . . . Cassie . . .

(AARON *fades. The lights come up on* MAJESKI *in the portrait, laughing softly, but malevolently.*)

MAJESKI: Suffer! You must suffer!

(MARY *and* CASSIE *regard each other for a short beat. Then* MARY *sits back in her wheel chair. She and* CASSIE, *again, regard each other for a short beat.*)

MARY: Breakfast! I will take breakfast . . . now! And don't you dare overcook my egg! You hear me?

(MARY *wheels herself into her room closing the door behind herself.* CASSIE, *wearily, leaves the room and goes toward the kitchen.* MAJESKI'S *laugh grows in volume until it seems to fill the room, then fades. All lights fade, except that behind the PORTRAIT. Then it, too, goes out.*)

END

Dame Lorraine

Dame Lorraine was first produced at the Victory Gardens Theater in Chicago on 27 March 1981. Chuck Smith directed the following cast:

RENIE MOULINEAUX . . . . Jackie Taylor
ANGELA MOULINEAUX . . . . Linda Bright
SALVATORE BUONGUSTO . . . . Vince Viverito
DORCAS MOULINEAUX . . . . Esther Rolle
PICTON MOULINEAUX . . . . Don Xerique Williams

Thomas Beall designed the set; Kate Bergh, the costumes; and John Rodriguez, the lighting.

To Vi (together . . . wherever) and
the one and only, "Yaya", Mrs. Alice Honoré,

and

Special, grateful thanks
to Esther Rolle,
The Empress

The great actress . . . the great friend

Characters

PICTON MOULINEAUX

DORCAS MOULINEAUX

ANGELA MOULINEAUX

RENIE MOULINEAUX

SALVATORE BUONGUSTO

ACT ONE

(An immaculate, but modestly furnished apartment in Harlem. Visible are that portion of the dimly lit hallway just outside the apartment door, the living room, the kitchen, and a good portion of the larger bedroom. RENIE MOULINEAUX *is alone in the kitchen having coffee and humming softly along with the hymns that emanate from a radio broadcast of Sunday morning church services.* ANGELA MOULINEAUX *and* SAL BUONGUSTO *appear in the hall, and she knocks on the door.* RENIE *immediately turns off the radio and stands, motionless.* ANGELA, *agitatedly, knocks again.* RENIE *walks through the living room and stands, silently, at the door.* ANGELA *knocks again.)*

ANGELA: Open the door. . . . Someone . . . open the door.

RENIE: Who is it?

ANGELA: Angela.

RENIE: Who?

ANGELA: Angela!

SAL: *(To himself)* Just Angela.

ANGELA: Open the door. There's no light out here . . .

RENIE: Oh!

*(*RENIE *unlocks to admit* ANGELA, *who darts inside.)*

ANGELA: The bell downstairs . . . doesn't it work? I just pushed the door and came in and walked up . . .

*(*SAL, *to* RENIE's *bewilderment, steps in.)*

RENIE: 'Scuse me. I didn't see you.

SAL: That's nothing new.

ANGELA: This bell doesn't work either.

RENIE: They're sometime-y. Sometimes they work. Sometimes . . . they don't. I guess today . . . they don't! Figures . . .!

ANGELA: And the lights. What happened to the lights in the hall? It's so dark.

SAL: Relax!

ANGELA: Relax? Relax? The cab driver didn't even want to bring me up here . . . and he was black, mind you. I guess if I didn't look like I look, he wouldn't have picked me up in the first place. Then when I do get here . . . it looks like World War VIII. What happened to all the buildings? They're shells. Just shells. Is this the only building on the block that's still alive? And who are all those . . . things just standing there . . . looking evil?

RENIE: . . . Just junkies . . .

ANGELA: Oh . . . I'm sorry. It's just that . . .

RENIE: You don't have to apologize or explain . . .

ANGELA: This is Sal Buongusto. This is my sister-in-law . . Well, how stupid of me. You two would have to know each other, wouldn't you?

SAL: Sure would.

RENIE: Went all the way through elementary school together . . .

SAL: For openers. How are you, Irene? Only it was Renie then.

RENIE: My name was never "Irene". It was "Reine".

SAL: That's right. French for "queen". . . .

RENIE: Y'all thought it sounded "Dictey", and just called me "Renie". "Renie", "Irene", "Reine". Same letters, only scrambled around some. Guess I am sort of an anagram, at that.

SAL: But you used to always say you were a queen and would marry a king when you grew up. . . . and you did.

RENIE: Found out there could only be one queen in this family and as for how I am . . . well . . . I'm here.

ANGELA: I suppose my mother's at church . . .

RENIE: It's Sunday . . . ain't it?

ANGELA: (*Under*) Oh, God!

RENIE: She's okay. Ain't none of them going to bother her. Besides . . . she's with some neighbors. So, Sal. It's been a long time. I ain't seen you since . . .

SAL: . . . in a long time . . .

Renie: Yeah! Ma told me the two of you had hooked up. Just goes to show you how small this world is . . .

Sal: Just shows to go you . . .

Renie: Believe it or not, we went together for about two . . . three minutes in the third or fourth grade. Can't remember which. Some little, jealous pissy-tail girlfriend of mine come telling me his folks . . . come telling me some lie or the other . . . so I quit him and she went with him . . .

Sal: For about two . . . three minutes . . .

Renie: What was that girl's name . . . Janice something or the other.

Sal: Who wants to remember back that far . . . ?

Renie: We used to be pretty nasty to you in school . . .

Sal: All kids are pretty nasty to each other in school. Forget it!

Renie: Yeah! So . . . Angela?

Angela: So . . . Irene?

Renie: Your mother keeps me up to date on all the plays you been in . . . All the commercials and stuff . . .

Angela: Then she can't have too much to say to you. I've been in two commercials . . .

Renie: Never saw'em. Teevee's broke. Been meaning to get it fixed, but don't seem to be any great need. Always figured you to grow up to be an actress or something like that . . .

Sal: Or something like that. Even then she knew . . .

Angela: Sal says it's a profession where you're always looking for a job. Sal says it's a profession where women get paid for convincing men they mean it when they say . . .

Sal and Angela: "I love you" . . .

Sal: . . . You see, Irene, I say a lot of things . . .

(Renie *notices* Angela *looking toward the large bedroom.*)

Renie: He's in there.

Angela: How is he?

Renie: Comes and goes. In and out. One minute . . . talking sense. The next . . . off in another time somewhere. . . . Doesn't really make much difference.

ANGELA: You think it would be okay if I opened the door and . . .

RENIE: Why're you asking me?

ANGELA: I don't know. I feel I have to . . .

RENIE: Well, you don't. He's your father.

ANGELA: But a stranger. My father. . . . My mother. . . . Strangers to me. Thirty years since I've seen him. Thirty years since I've been in this house. . . . In this room. Thirty years . . I don't even realize how long it's been until I hear myself saying it. Nothing but beds in this room then. All those beds . . . in this one room.

SAL: You gonna stand rooted to that spot forever? Why don't you sit down . . . someplace?

ANGELA: They wouldn't let me come back. Don't you see? I couldn't come back. So you're their daughter now. This is your house. I have to ask you if I can go in and see him. I have to ask you if I can. . . .

RENIE: You don't have to ask me nothing. This place is yours whenever you want it. You can keep the vigil too.

ANGELA: I couldn't come back. They wouldn't let me . .

RENIE: Look, have some coffee. Damn! Don't know why people think a cup of coffee cures everything. Maybe you want something stronger . . .?

SAL: Something stronger for me!

RENIE: There's some elderberry wine over there.

SAL: Coffee will be fine!

ANGELA: I'll go in and look at him.

(RENIE and SAL go into the kitchen . . . leaving ANGELA. SAL pours himself a cup of coffee . . . and one for ANGELA.)

SAL: I've this feeling this is the safest thing to drink.

(ANGELA comes into the kitchen. SAL hands her the cup.)

SAL: Your folks still alive, Renie?

ANGELA: Oh! I'm sorry. My mother told me about your father . . .

RENIE: Couldn't even find enough of him left to put next to my mama in that hole. I said some words for him and let it go at that. Cheap bastard. His own fault. All he had to do was hire an electrician or somebody. Well, both of them can stay dead . . . for all I care. Never had nothing for me after I got pregnant with Freddie. Didn't particularly like them anyway. Well, they're gone now. My brother too. Did you know that? Died fighting in some country or the other for money. All the free death they handing out on the street and he had to go buy his. He could've had it free just like Freddie. Freddie was born to die. Funny . . . I was never happy with him. Damn sure wasn't happy having him. Even said to myself when I first saw him, "This is an overdose if ever there was one!" Y'all want cream for your coffee?

ANGELA: What time is it?

SAL: Your watch stop?

RENIE: There's a big clock right there. Listen, I know you're nervous and edgy. Me, too. Can't help but be . . . but today ain't going no faster than yesterday. No faster. No slower.

ANGELA: I shouldn't have come. Why did I come here?

RENIE: Ma didn't want you to, but she knew you had to. Ask yourself how were you not going to come here this day.

ANGELA: I couldn't put it off. Isn't that what you said, Sal?

SAL: You knew you had to come. Just like I know I had to come.

(*From the bedroom . . . an ear-splitting scream.*)

PICTON: DORCAS!

(SAL *and* ANGELA *jump up simultaneously.*)

SAL: Good God!

ANGELA: What's wrong?

(ANGELA *is running toward the door.* SAL *stops her.*)

What's wrong with him?

RENIE: The nightmare! Just . . . the nightmare.

SAL: Like father, like daughter. You'd think, by now, I'd recognize a good, old-fashioned nightmare right off . . . wouldn't you, Angela?

ANGELA: I want to see him!

SAL: Don't you think you ought to wait and let him come out of it by himself? I'm not without some experience in these matters . . .

ANGELA: I want to see him?

SAL: Hey! Do what you have to . . .

(SAL *sits and continues to drink his coffee.* ANGELA *starts out defiantly for the bedroom, but falters as she nears the door. She slowly opens it and peers in. Stifling a scream, she closes the door and runs to the entry door, but the several locks give her difficulty.* SAL *clutches and holds her.*)

ANGELA: Let me go! Let me go!

SAL: It's okay.

ANGELA: He's bones! He's skin and bones! That's not my father! All that's left for that old thing in there to do . . . is die. That's not my father!

SAL: Easy! I'm here. Easy, now. I'm here. You know I'm here. You know it!

ANGELA: Oh, Sal. Where's my daddy? My daddy's gone.

RENIE: Take her into my room.

(SAL *leads* ANGELA *toward the room.*)

RENIE: Look under my pillow. There's a little scotch there.

SAL: Thanks!

RENIE: I only keep it for my own nightmares. Soon! Everybody's nightmares'll be over. Soon!

SAL: One way or the other . . .

(SAL *takes* ANGELA *into* RENIE'S *room.*)

(*A little later.* RENIE *sits in the kitchen.* DORCAS MOULINEAUX *comes to the landing and calls to someone downstairs.*)

DORCAS: Okay. I reach.

(*She knocks at the door. Again, as before,* RENIE *is apprehensive, but before she can get too deeply into it,* DORCAS *knocks again.*)

DORCAS: Renie, is me. Open, nuh.

(RENIE *opens the door to admit this woman of 84 years.*)

DORCAS: Damn fool, me! I getting anile! I get quite to my pew before I realize I ain't have pocketbook, the first. Everybody see I ain't put nothing in the plate. Couldn't even fake it. Come-what-you-bet my name in everybody mouth before the day out. Lord. Too much on my mind. Too much. Anything happen?

RENIE: She's in my room.

DORCAS: She alone?

RENIE: No.

DORCAS: Oh, God!

RENIE: He's a good man, Ma.

DORCAS: He not the right man. Not for her. Not with the thing between them. I ain't care how good she say he is to her, he can't be good for her.

RENIE: It's between them.

DORCAS: Is between all of us. You in it too.

RENIE: They're still each other's business.

DORCAS: I guess is just one more thing to worry me. Well, how she look?

RENIE: Still look like a younger version of you.

DORCAS: I know she pretty, but how she look?

RENIE: Good.

DORCAS: She ain't seem . . . edgy?

RENIE: When she came in . . .

DORCAS: I knew I should've been here. I should have follow me mind and not go to church today. I ain't think she would come so early. I should have follow me mind.

RENIE: She's okay. He's taking care of her.

DORCAS: She see she father? What she say when she see him? What he do? What he say to she? I know I should've been here.

RENIE: He didn't wake up. She didn't say too much. We sort of skirted around things. Like you and me. How come we can't just talk about things and get it over with?

DORCAS: We still have time.

RENIE: You always say that. You been saying it for . . .

DORCAS: Well, we still do . . .

RENIE: No, we don't! Today is here!

DORCAS: Later, Darlin'. Later.

RENIE: Ma. Today is here!

(*At* RENIE's *louder tone,* ANGELA *opens the bedroom door.*)

DORCAS: I going start breakfast. Is good she sleeping. When she was a little girl . . . before . . . before. . . . She always like to wake up to the smell of my biscuits baking in the oven. "Is the best smell in the whole, wide, world, Moomah."

(ANGELA *and* SAL *come out of the bedroom.*)

ANGELA: It still is.

DORCAS: Oh!

(DORCAS *and* ANGELA *look at each other for a moment. For their own reasons, they are unable to embrace.*)

DORCAS: I never thought to see you in this house again. I ain't want to see you here . . . but I too glad you come. You have to understand . . . we had to stay here and my place was with him. I just a woman. You have to understand. I was doing what I thought best.

ANGELA: Don't take yourself through this again. You've said all this before.

DORCAS: But it mean more now that you really here. But you going see. After today, you going see. My little baby girl. I going make it all up to you.

ANGELA: There's nothing to make up. Mother.

DORCAS: Well, that bring me down. When you call me, "Mother", so . . . it sound like a knife. I long for them day when you call me, "Moomah". Oh, well. My fault. Let me go in the kitchen. We all going need to eat this day.

SAL: Hello, Mrs. Moulineaux.

DORCAS: How are you, young man?

SAL: Fine, thank you. Kind of you to ask, M'am. And you?

DORCAS: Is what you see here. Your people still 'live? Angela never say.

SAL: Never really talk about them. My mother left here in the early '60's. Went back home.

DORCAS: I forget she was from home.

SAL: I heard she died.

DORCAS: Where she was from?

SAL: One of the islands. Never knew which.

DORCAS: Where your father?

SAL: I heard he went back to Italy. I think he's still alive.

DORCAS: Must be as old as the ruins. Well, he was always fair with me. Always bring me a big piece of ice for my money. Could always run up a bill and pay him at the end of every fortnight. I ain't even want to tell him when we get our first refrigerator. He was something, that one. I know three . . . four girls who make baby for him, but he always respect me. Oh! 'Scuse me.

SAL: The old story, I guess. The iceman cometh . . . several times . . . it would seem, and the iceman runneth away. Well, at least he wasn't deported, eh? Old Italian joke . . . there.

(RENIE *starts to laugh.*)

SAL: I guess it is kind of funny . . . at that.

RENIE: Not laughing at you, Sal. It's things. All of a sudden things seem funny. Don't they seem funny to you? To none of you? Lord, who would've thought that all our lives would be tied up with one neat ribbon. All these different lives.

SAL: I don't think we had any say about that . . .

RENIE: And even that don't strike you funny?

DORCAS: All right, Renie.

RENIE: Why won't you talk about it?

DORCAS: 'Cause I don't have to. I know what's coming. I just don't know what I going do. I ain't know what to do. You know what you going do? You make up you mind what you going tell him when he come? You think I ain't had nothing to do all these years. It on my mind every minute. Too many things on my mind, girl. Young man, I always look down on you mother and you father and all them girl he get in trouble. But in the long run, I ain't no different. Me and my Picton just the same as you folks. We come to this country, have all the children we can and mess up they life.

ANGELA: . . . That's not so . . .

DORCAS: . . . and mess up they life and then . . . run off back home like some thief in the night. We just the same. Is the end result that count. Who say, "No!"? That what me and Picton going do, you know. After all this thing settle, we going home and die. We going try to be under a palm tree when it come. We should never come here. . . . But, hear me, nuh? Chatter! Chatter! Chatter! All you must be starve.

PICTON: (*From within*) *Dorcas Moulineaux!*

DORCAS: Hear him, nuh! The master's voice!

PICTON: You ain't hear me pronounce your name?

DORCAS: What you want, your high and mightiness?

PICTON: You keeping too much noise. I trying to get my beauty sleep.

DORCAS: You would have to sleep your lifetime and mine . . .

PICTON: What you say? What you say?

DORCAS: I no talk plain?

PICTON: Me mother warn me against you, you know. She said you was a tyrant. Make I come out there and behead you.

DORCAS: Executioner, you better keep that old axe in your pant where it belong.

PICTON: Mother, God rest your bones, you hear how she talk vicious to me? You hear how the criminal flog me with she tongue. I coming out there to give you one good t'ump. You better run. And when I through, I want me breakfast.

DORCAS: Virago*, you think I is maid servant? Come out and see what you get! But you better wash you mouth and brush you teeth and don't forget to emp you pochamb. I don't feed no man who ain't clean. Don't let him kiss me neither.

PICTON: Woman, you so raucous. Is no wonder I too love you. (*He prepares to come out.*)

DORCAS: That man could always make me forget I have so much trouble. I ain't want nothing said to make he upset. All you got that? All right now!

(PICTON *comes out carrying his chamber pot.*)

PICTON: Woman, why you mouth so foul? You should. . . . Oh! I ain't know we have guest. Dawkie, why you no tell me . . . and me with me pot. Pardon, me, pretty lady. I hope you ain't mind me saying, Mister, but you have one pretty wife. Almost pretty like mine. You know, she look just like somebody I use to . . . We ain't meet before, Mistress? You favor somebody I know. Long ago. . . . Long ago. . . . I ain't remember.

DORCAS: Picton, is Angela. Angela! You baby come home. Remember how you always say, "That little angel too make a fool out of me."? Remember? Is she. She come home to you.

PICTON: You will all excuse me, please. I can't receive today. We all going out this evening. We all going to Dame Lorraine.

---

*Pronounced "vī-rā-guh"

ANGELA: Daddy, it's me! Look at me! Look at me!

DORCAS: All right now! I warn you!

PICTON: You and you man welcome to come along . . . if you like, but we can't entertain nobody here just now. We have to get ready. I would show you me costume but, I want it to take everybody by surprise. In case you ain't know, I leading The Immaculate Marauder Band. Yes! I going be The Grand High Invader for the tenth year in a row. Nobody beat that record. But don't you tell a soul who it is. You hear?

ANGELA: Daddy, it's me!

DORCAS: You hear?

ANGELA: I . . . won't tell a soul . . .

PICTON: I charge you!

ANGELA: I promise.

PICTON: I tired now. I going to me room. I going rest up for tonight. If you decide to come along, I promise you one, big time.

ANGELA: Would you like me. . . . Would you like some help.

PICTON: I ain't invalid, you know. Beside, if my wife see you touch me . . . there would be particular hell to pay. She jealous, you know. I did have a little girl once. She dead! (*He totters back to his room.*)

DORCAS: He ain't mean that. I never tell him that. He ain't mean to hurt you.

ANGELA: It's okay. I'm not hurt.

SAL: She said . . . lying to herself.

RENIE: The world is full of us fools who do . . .

DORCAS: He act like he ain't know you, but he know you. I keep every picture you ever take and he see them. Deep down, he know you. He just need time. The man ain't been able to look you in the face for thirty years. He need some time . . . is all.

SAL: Thirty years isn't enough time?

DORCAS: He need more.

PICTON: (*From within*) Dawkie! Dawkie! Come quick! I need you, Dawkie!

ANGELA: What's the matter?

RENIE: He needs her!

DORCAS: (*To God*) I just come from church. I just get through talking with you. Why you want to do this to me? Why you sitting up there planning all sort of thing to ruin this moment for me? Why you can't take me now? Why you don't take me this minute while I here with the three people I love in all the world? Why you no take me now so they is the last thing I see? Why you have to ruin thing by letting this day go on? Oh, sometime you is such a cruel God .. and I can't understand you at all . . . (*She goes into the bedroom.*)

ANGELA: Sal, I can't take this. I can't go through with this. Let's get out of here.

SAL: Ah! So now it's "let's", is it?

ANGELA: It's getting late . . .

SAL: Angela, sit down!

ANGELA: I'm going.

SAL: Sit down or go into Irene's room and lie down. I don't care whether or not you go to sleep . . . but you do something. You're just not leaving here.

ANGELA: . . . but . . . I don't want to stay . . .

SAL: You have to. I have to.

RENIE: We all have to, girl. He know we'll all be here. No use running away from it. I've been running for the last twenty-seven years. Stayed right here in this apartment and been running all that time. It's time I stopped.

SAL: It's time we all stopped. It's time we all settled up and got what's ours.

ANGELA: I don't know what that is. I mean . . . just what is that supposed to be? What's ours?

SAL: When King Moulineaux walks through that door . . . you'll know.

RENIE: Guess we'll all know. . . . Won't we?

(ANGELA *goes into* RENIE'S *room and slams the door behind her.*)

SAL: Che sará, sará! Believe it or not, aside from my name, that is just about all the Italian I know. Now, ain't that a shame!

(*Lights up on* DORCAS *and* PICTON.)

PICTON: Dawkie, hold me.

DORCAS: Yes, Darlin'.

PICTON: Close.

DORCAS: Yes, Darlin'.

PICTON: So close and so tight, it feel like you squeezing your life right into me.

DORCAS: Yes, Darlin'.

PICTON: In all the years since I first see you, I ain't even know other woman was in this world. You know that?

DORCAS: Yes, Darlin'.

PICTON: When I die, I hope I have enough strength to kneel over and kiss you feet. That the last thing I ever want to do in this life. You been everything to me. You been my wife. You been my friend. You been my shield and protector. Oh, Dawkie, you been my God. I too love you.

DORCAS: Yes, Darlin'.

PICTON: Dawkie, that was our baby all grow up so?

DORCAS: Yes, Darlin'.

PICTON: Why? I ain't want her to see me. I too shame. I ain't want her to see me. Why she come? Why she come?

DORCAS: She have to. That is all.

PICTON: But she not safe here. This place have bad spirit waitin' for her. Bad people in this world waiting to hurt her. There's things I never tell you, Darlin'. I ain't want to see you upset and cry.

DORCAS: I ain't matter. But nobody going hurt our little girl again.

PICTON: You promise?

DORCAS: And nobody goin' hurt you neither. Your Dawkie going make everything all right. And then . . . soon . . . very soon . . . you and me going do just like we always say. We going buy them ticket and go home. Just like we always say.

PICTON: That sound so good. But first, one more Dame Lorraine. We go to one more Dame Lorraine. . . . Then we go right from Rockland Palace to the boat. How that sound?

DORCAS: Oh, Doux-doux, you know I always do anything you want me to . . .

PICTON: I know, one more Dame Lorraine . . . then . . . home. You know is only good things happen when we go to Dame Lorraine. One more. . . . One more . . .

PICTON AND DORCAS: . . . then . . . home!

PICTON: . . . and we could finish up there, Honey-girl?

DORCAS: What else?

PICTON: Girl . . . I too love you.

DORCAS: Yes, Darlin'.

(*Lights down on* PICTON *and* DORCAS.)

END ACT ONE

ACT TWO

(*Later.* SAL *and* RENIE *in the kitchen, doing dishes.*)

RENIE: That's the last of them. Thanks.

SAL: Nothing to it. Thanks for the breakfast.

RENIE: Things didn't work quite like Ma wanted. She wanted to fix a really nice breakfast . . . for Angela.

SAL: Well, it was enough. It's not exactly a festive occasion, is it?

RENIE: Sal?

SAL: Yeah?

RENIE: I couldn't look you in the face during the trial. I felt like you blamed me along with him.

SAL: I did. I blamed all of you Moulineaux.

RENIE: Is that why you're with Angela. Is she part of your plan to get back at us?

SAL: Is that what you think?

RENIE: It's what Ma thinks.

SAL: It's what she's always thought . . .

RENIE: Is she right?

SAL: Angela and I are another story.

RENIE: Don't spoil it for yourself, Sal.

SAL: Meaning?

RENIE: You made it. You got out of here. You made your life count for something.

SAL: Ha! Irene, I'm nothing special. A house painter. One of the best, mind you and I can overcharge with the best of them . . . but. . . . I'm a house painter . . . nevertheless. You would think, wouldn't you, that with this Italian blood coursing through my veins, I'd have been another Michelangelo . . . da Vinci . . . or Raffaello. No I'm a house painter. Only one of them I ever hear tell "made his life count for something" was Hitler.

RENIE: You killed anybody lately? You been sitting in a jail for twenty seven years? You ever beat the shit out of your wife and son? You ever rape your sister? You ever beat your father . . . senseless . . .

SAL: Now . . . there's a thought.

RENIE: You made it. In spite of everything, you made it. I'm still waiting. Don't be like me. Don't throw it all away and be like me. I remember you at the trial. Screaming for vengeance . . .

SAL: . . . vendetta!

RENIE: . . . swearing to kill him . . .

SAL: . . . vendetta! You got to know what my sister meant to me. The way we had to cling together was special to me. You decent folks kept pointing your whole fingers and calling us "half-nigger" one minute and "half-wop" the next. You got any idea what it's like to be just a half of anything? I'd see my whole Italian father delivering ice to you whole colored folks and he wouldn't speak to me . . . except to call me a "half-nigger". What the fuck did he think I was going to be? But dig this. When you found out that Carla was fooling around with King and y'all had that fight . . . she told me the only worthwhile thing to come out of it was that you called her a whore. She actually appreciated it because you didn't call her a "half-nigger whore". "At last", she said, "to be something . . . whole." The next day . . . he killed her. Our father didn't come to her funeral or the trial. Neither did her mother. They were united in that.

RENIE: You could've been one of us anytime you wanted. Person looking like you . . . they're anything they say they are. You didn't want to be black. You wanted to be . . .

SAL: I wanted to be whole, damn it. Whole! Couldn't nobody understand it then. Can't nobody understand it now. Whole!

RENIE: Whole! Hah! Tell me about it. I was only a half a person. Only felt whole when King came to me. Always had it for King Moulineaux.

My mama wasn't no different from all the other mothers 'round here. "Stay 'way from those Moulineaux boys. All eight of them got the bad seed. They the devil. Even they own mama can't explain 'em." Could not hear her! He was flame! Me? Moth! When I got pregnant, he actually married me. Never could figure out, "Why?" Other guys did the "right thing", sure. But he was a Moulineaux. Moulineaux never did what other guys did. I don't know. Maybe he was trying to make a stab at being decent. I don't know. The baby came and he left. That I could understand. Then he started coming by the place and kicking my behind. Sometimes, he wouldn't say a word. Just come by and immediately start kicking my behind. Little Freddie would cry sometimes . . . and he would start knocking him around. I used to wonder why he was so damn evil. That face of his would . . . sort of . . . hypnotize me into doing nothing. Dumb me . . . I always thought anybody who was colored and that good looking had to be happy . . . you know? Then I started thinking . . . maybe he was that evil 'cause he was that good looking and wasn't white. Well, who knows? Anyway . . . after he killed . . . your sister, he comes to my place to . . . what? Hide out? Rest? I don't know. And without so much as a, "By your leave . . .", that nigger started giving my behind a beating. By this time, Little Freddie was too smart to cry, so he stood there . . . looking and not saying a word. How he managed to get the knife to me, is still a mystery. How I managed to stick it in him was even more of a mystery. . . . God, his face looked even more handsome while he was trying to kill me. But I stabbed him. He made a lunge to get at Little Freddie, but he side-stepped. King just sort of laid there . . . trying to get . . . trying to reach for him. He knew Freddie wasn't helping me . . . but was getting even for his own sake. I went to the police station. Left Freddie there to watch him. Swore he'd be dead by the time I got back. He wasn't. It went downhill from there. By the time Freddie was eleven, he was hooked. Before he was twelve, he was gone. I never cried. Haven't yet. That part was over. . . . I thought. Now, they letting him out and he's coming here and demand to know why I let his son die and why I never came to see him. . . . Like he was some good husband and father and I spilled his precious blood. I know I'm going to see that face and go soft all over. I know it. I ain't had nobody. . . . I just need somebody. . . . Sal, help me.

SAL: Me?

RENIE: We ain't strangers. Our lives are tied together. Help me. Stand by me. Help me be strong. For my sake . . . help me!

SAL: For your sake! For Angela's sake! For the sake of my sister . . . may she rest in peace. . . . Now, do I hear anybody who wants to make me be strong for my sake? Come on! Let's hear it for me!

DORCAS: There's always God. Thanks for washing the dishes, young man, but you ain't have to.

SAL: I know that. Angela okay?

DORCAS: She in there with him. Just looking at him. Once in a while, he look at her. Can't say nothing. Trying to look away thirty years. I couldn't stay. I feel I ain't belong.

RENIE: I'm suffocating. You need anything from the store? I'm going out.

DORCAS: Where?

RENIE: I won't be gone long. Be back in plenty of time.

DORCAS: Be careful.

RENIE: Don't worry. Bring you back some cherry-vanilla. (*To* SAL) One of her true pleasures.

DORCAS: She going a couple few blocks and stand in front of the place where she and King lived for a while. My grandson die in that place. She just going stand in front and look at it, then she going to the church and sit in the back and wish she could cry. She a good woman, but she simple. She love evil. She feel guilty 'cause she love evil. I make her my daughter 'cause is me bring the evil she love into the world. I make her my daughter and make my own stay away from this place . . . 'cause I know my daughter fascinated by evil . . . too. Poor Angela. You love her?

SAL: Yes.

DORCAS: You ain't have some other purpose in mind? Why you love her?

SAL: Why does anybody love anybody? You're right to suspect me. I'll admit it started out for other reasons. But, I guess, in the long run . . . It was just fate. Like everything else. I didn't know her when I lived around her. She wasn't my age group and I just didn't pay her no mind. Just kind of bumped into her at this party a couple of years ago . . . I didn't plan it. . . . But then you know all this. Anyway, after I found out who she was. . . . Pow! It leaped into my mind. "Her brother killed your sister. Why not kill his . . . in some way." Once she loved me, make her life too miserable to live. The rest is difficult for me because I mean you no disrespect. As you know, whenever you come to see her . . . I stay away from the place because I respect your views . . . but you did ask. The first time Angela and I went . . . went to bed together. . . . That's when I found out. You can believe it or not, Mrs. Moulineaux, but I've not bothered her since then. No! I'm neither a saint or a patient man. I have other women. For some reason, I love Angela. It's been two years ... but maybe after today ... if we go together again, she'll see my face and not her brother's.

DORCAS: You are a patient man. None of the others was patient with her. They ain't care. They take her and after they beat her. . . . Then they cast her aside. . . . She have to have it that way. . . . Then she stay alone alot. It too tragic ... and too funny all at the same time and I never going understand it. I too simple. My brain ain't make for such thing. Only thing I ever do well is love that okd stick in there. But I do everything God ask me to and ... behold me . . Seven boys gone out of eight. The last one coming home just now. My only grandson ... gone. You will excuse me 'cause I ain't mean you no insult, but the truth is the light. You mother never see the inside of a church. You father plaster the block with his leavings ...

SAL: ... hah! ...

DORCAS: ... I live in the church and try to do good. My husband is a good man. He never spend one night away from me. But, together, we bring eight devil and loose them on the world. You folks get you. You can figure it out?

SAL: Nothing to figure out. What will be ...

DORCAS AND SAL: ... will be ...

DORCAS: ... I know, but all the same ... when I see God ... and that going be soon, I guess. . . . I going ask him what the hell he had in mind ... 'cause it all too slip by me.

SAL: I guess there's still a lot more we have to say to each other, but I'm glad we had this little talk. Glad some things are out in the open.

DORCAS: After tonight, please God, things going be different. Angela going be free in she mind. So, tomorrow morning, you don't go to work. Stay home with her. She forty-two. Is about time she find out a man can feel damn good when he doing what he do best. After that, you have plenty time for being in love.

ANGELA: He's asleep. Scared me a little. He just drifted off with this strange look on his face ... then he smiled. . . . For a minute, I thought. . . . He looked that peaceful.

DORCAS: I going to him. Angela?

ANGELA: Yes?

DORCAS: I do a bad thing sending you to you aunt when you come out the hospital.

ANGELA: Don't go into that now.

DORCAS: When we come in and see those three boys on you ... all I could think about was to get you away so you wouldn't be hurt.

ANGELA: Don't do this to yourself. To me.

DORCAS: Is my memory. Who else live with it? The man ain't have the strength to beat them. His heart break and he couldn't even feel proper rage. After they pummel him so, he cry out, "Dawkie, help me. My sons killing me!" I fling myself across him. I fight my way in there and fling my body right across him. They pick me up and pitch me aside like an old rag. They mother! When I wake up .. oh .. what I find? I ain't think he have blood left in him. It seem I was cleaning him for hours. They leave me that ... in there. Thirty years of ... that ... in there. I should have kill them, but I hear God voice telling me he going do it. One by one, he strike them down. But, God, is thirty years and the worse one still 'live to do menace. The worse one coming through that door soon. God, you too slow. In the meantime, Darling, I cheat you. In my way .. I cheat you. We send you from here to keep you out they way.

ANGELA: I know ...

DORCAS: No ... you ain't. We send you away ... because when we come in and see them all over you ... and the others laughing ... we also see the look of pleasure on you face.

ANGELA: No!

DORCAS: We see it!

ANGELA: No!

DORCAS: You father see it. He see it ... and it break his heart. .... The others kill him when they t'ump him ... but he ain't feel it because he was dead already ...

ANGELA: No! No! No! I'm not a monster!

DORCAS: We no blame you, girl. We know it all our fault. We make you. You come from us. .... So we send you away. I cheat you. I keep you from being one with this man. After tonight, take them cloud from inside you head. Hold this man. He remind me of you father ... before ... before. .... I cheat myself, too. You can't call me, "Moomah".

(DORCAS *goes to her room. Lights out.*)

(*A bit later.*)

SAL: What do you think she'll wear out first, folks ... the carpet or herself?

ANGELA: I'm just worried about Renie walking around in this neighborhood.

SAL: Yeah!

ANGELA: You saw all those misfits looking at us when we got out of the cab. Sunday morning and all those . . . things . . . just standing there. Hanging out. You saw them. Driver couldn't even wait for a tip. And Renie's out there by herself.

SAL: I take it you want me to believe you're worried about Renie.

ANGELA: I am.

SAL: Renie can take care of herself.

ANGELA: I'm worried all the same.

SAL: Angela, I don't know what's going to happen today, but beginning tomorrow . . . no more lying to yourself. No more telling yourself things to cover up the truth. If you do, you'll have to do it without me. If that's what it takes, I'm willing.

ANGELA: Casting me out, are you?

SAL: No! Casting me out.

ANGELA: I wondered how long you'd wait. I wondered how long it'd be before you proved you were like the others. I've been waiting two years for it.

SAL: Shut your damned mouth. Again, you confuse me with other men. Again, you think all I've ever wanted from you is a . . . piece of ass. Well, it's time we were quits if I've failed to convince you that you're more than just a woman to me. I'm over fifty years old. All I've ever done with women is go in, grunt and get gone. You want to know how boring that can get to be. All I've ever heard was, "Was it good?", "Was I the best?", "Did you like it, Honey?" and leave us not forget the ever-popular, "Oooooooweee, Baby!" There ought to be more! There's got to be more! Just once, I'd like to have somebody who is not above or below looking me in the eye. Let me look back into hers while silent messages just . . . flow. I can't help it if I need someone's arms around me when I have to cry. You think you're the only one who. . . . Damn it! I wish this bastard would come the hell on so we can get this shit over and done with . . . one way or the other.

ANGELA: You insisted on coming. I didn't want you to.

SAL: I've said all I'm going to say.

ANGELA: Well, what do you want me to say? I can't blame you. You've been patient but, remember, I've always said you shouldn't bother about me. I've always said you should go. You think I don't feel hatred for myself because I'm glad you're with them and not me? I do. I'm all sham and I know it. I can't help myself and, as I've tried to tell you so many times, neither can you. They knew I still wasn't feeling well that night. I don't know. I seemed to be on fire one minute and freezing the next. I don't know. I just wasn't feeling right. Hah! Just a girl getting over the humiliation of a first period. Nothing to get wound up about. It was Dame Lorraine night and Daddy wasn't going to miss it. Mother didn't want to go, but Daddy said, "All the fuss over and, beside, she twelve. Old enough to stay by sheself". Blame it on that! Blame it on the fever! Blame it on whatever you want. I was sort of walking around with practically nothing on. I heard the door open. King! To this day, I don't know what made me just stand there . . . looking at him. He grabbed me and. . . . I never screamed. He was looking into my eyes all the time. Sal, I was looking back. I could see myself. After a while, it didn't hurt. I didn't even know when the others came in. All of sudden they were . . . just . . . there . . . and he . . . offered me to them. Funny. . . . I can't even remember what the rest of them looked like. . . . Only him! Funny. I never screamed. I never said a word. Then . . . Daddy's face was there. He looked. . . . He looked like he was somewhere else. I had passed shame. I guess he had, too. Finally, I was able to scream and yell. Maybe it was seeing Daddy's face . . . but I did scream, "It wouldn't have happened if you'd stayed home with me . . . but you had to go to your damned Dame Lorraine." His eyes died right there. Leave Sal! I'm not acting now. Leave before you die. I kill people. I killed my father. I'll kill you. You want me to face truth and reality? Can you? Can you take it when I tell you that my mother was right. She read the truth in my face. No man has . . . ever . . . made . . . me feel the . . . the . . . something . . . I felt that night. The pain. . . . The horror. . . . The something . . . I felt that night. No man ever will again. That beating . . . as bad as it was . . . didn't do that to my father. I did it! I killed Him!

(DORCAS *comes out of the room with* ANGELA'S *purse.*)

DORCAS: And because you revile yourself so, who you bring this here to do? (*She takes a gun from* ANGELA'S *purse.*) You or you brother?

(ANGELA *lunges for the gun.* SAL *stops her.*)

ANGELA: Give it to me!

DORCAS: Or maybe is me and you father you want to kill 'cause we leave you 'lone that night.

ANGELA: Give it to me! Don't you see? I can't live until he dies.

DORCAS: You want to jook up the rest of your life, too? I ain't going have it. Is from me all this trouble spring. Is from this womb all them evil boy and you come.

SAL: Just calm down, Baby. Did you think I'd actually let you use it? Did you really think that? How little you really know me!

(RENIE *comes in.*)

RENIE: Hi! How's everybody? Brought you some cherry vanilla like I said. Hope it didn't melt to milk. Don't know what come over me. Just been dawdlin' in the hallway. Takin' my time. Comin' up the stairs. "Jus' amblin'", as they say in all those cowboy movies. Or is that, "Jus' moseyin'"? That's it! Just moseyin'! Ha!

SAL: You okay, Irene?

RENIE: Who? Me? Sure! I'm fine. I just decided. . . . No! Guess I knew all along. When King comes through that door and starts to carry out his threat to "beat my ass into the twenty-first century", for what "I did to him". . . . 'Scuse me, Ma, but I'm going to blow his ass away!

DORCAS: M'dear, you at the end of a long line!

(*The downstairs doorbell rings. Just one long, monotonous, incessant ring, which petrifies the four. The bell continues until the end of the scene.*)

PICTON: (*Screaming from the bedroom.*) Dawkie! Dawkie! Dawkie! Dawkie!

SAL: You bastard, I'm coming for you! (*He runs from the apartment.*)

PICTON: Dawkie! Dawkie! Dawkie! Dawkie, they killing me! My sons killing me!

(DORCAS *screams and runs into the room. The bell continues its long ring. Lights.*)

END ACT TWO

ACT THREE

(*Later, still. The apartment is empty and the door is open.* PICTON *is in the hallway looking over the railing and listening. Suddenly, he comes in and quickly (for him) goes to his room. He barely manages to get inside when there is a fumbling at the door.* RENIE, *followed by* ANGELA, *enters. They sit . . . saying nothing. After a bit,* SAL *enters, assisting* DORCAS *to a seat.* SAL *closes and locks the door. He goes into* RENIE'S *room and comes out with the scotch. He goes to the kitchen and comes back with four glasses, which he fills and hands, one each, to the women and keeps one for himself.*)

SAL: Drink it down! Fast!

(*They look at him, but do not drink. He does.*)

RENIE: His face! What did they do to his face in there? Nothing but old crusty skin and scars all over. What did they do to his face? His hair . . . scraggly white puffs of smoke. Patches of smoke and string. His body . . . used to be so . . . so. . . . I used to love. . . . No! That wasn't him. I got to go and tell them, "That wasn't him!"

(RENIE *goes for the door.* SAL *stops her.*)

SAL: They're gone, Renie. They've taken him away.

RENIE: But you don't understand. It wasn't him. It wasn't him. That thing leaning on the bell with his throat cut ear to ear . . . was not him. It was just another old man who got mugged. It wasn't him. It was just another old man. That's what they do nowdays, you know. They don't just rob you no more. They got to kill you, too. But nobody could do that to King Moulineaux. If that was King, he would know how to take care of himself. Anybody would be too scared to mess with King Moulineaux. It wasn't him!

ANGELA: It was him, God damn it! It was him!

RENIE: Well, if it was him . . . what did they do to his face? What did they do to him in there? What happened in there? (*She runs into her room.*)

DORCAS: At last . . . she cry. . . .

SAL: You okay?

ANGELA: I feel so . . . what's the word I'm looking for? Deflated? That's too simple. I thought I'd feel something . . . cooling. Like a breeze from the east or something. There's no breeze. There's . . . nothing. Damn it! I thought I'd be the one. I waited all these years . . . and some . . . nigger . . . junky . . . cheats me. I knew it when we drove up and saw them. I had this feeling. There's nothing left . . . is there, Sal? I don't feel . . . anything.

SAL: All the hatred gone?

ANGELA: I don't feel anything. I can't even feel the revulsion I have of myself. I can't feel anything . . . except . . . a fear. Yes! A fear! Sal, why am I afraid . . . now?

SAL: "I don't know", he said, lying to himself. Angela, baby . . . che sará, sará. Mrs. Moulineaux, can I do anything for you before I go? You want to go to your room, perhaps?

ANGELA: I still see his eyes . . .

DORCAS: . . . I'm all right.

ANGELA: . . . Those same eyes . . .

DORCAS: He was smiling. You see he had that smile on he face? He smile because he find out the street even more evil, now, than he. He smile because he own evil catch and surpass he. He smile because he know we all waiting for him and he cheat we. All gone! All gone! All my blood gone! The first and the last . . . gone! Eight boys born, eight boys gone! A reader tell me that once, you know. Eight boys born, eight boys gone! Hah! Sound like one of the calypso they does sing at the Dame Lorraine that old man in there always talk about. Well, it over now. That was the first and that was the last. I never want boys, you know. Never! All eight times was only salt, bile, and venom in my womb. By the time Angela finally come . . . all me sugar gone. Well, it over now and they all gone. What the police ain't kill . . . other people shoot and stab. And this one . . . prop up there with he throat cut . . . and all my blood run out. People always talk about me behind me back and say I just look bewildered all the time. And why not, if you please? I ain't never going understand it. Eight boys born! Eight boys gone! You can figure it out?

SAL: I still think you ought to rest.

ANGELA: She's all right, Sal.

DORCAS: Yes, Salvatore, my son, I'm all right. I need a little time to figure things out 'cause it look like God ain't going help me, but I'm all right. Besides, I going get plenty rest soon.

SAL: If you say so.

DORCAS: I ain't have no say.

(PICTON *emerges from the room. The others watch him. He takes up the wine carafe.*)

PICTON: But, Dawkie, all the wine gone?

DORCAS: Yes. All the wine gone . . . now.

PICTON: Well, we ain't need none. I have a feeling is only you and me going to Dame Lorraine tonight. Hello, young man. Ain't I know you? Ain't you the iceman boy? I know you. You ain't remember me, eh? I bet you know my boys. Everybody know my boys. Them boys . . . legend. Oh, Dawkie . . . I hear it. I hear the music. Listen! You ain't hear it? Listen!

Dum de dum de dum de dum de dee

No! Don't stop the carnival . . .

You hear it, young man? Happy time coming. Dame Lorraine coming. MacBeth the Great . . . he face ain't move a muscle . . . yet he singing for all he worth. Duke of Iron, with he long self . . . picking quatro and making it sound like one whole symphony band. Wilmouth Houdini with he voice dry like copper and Lord Invader singing like golden sand. They ain't know when for stop. Suddenly, the lights in Rockland Palace go down. People ain't know what happening, but they no make noise . . . they no panic. They quiet. Like mouse. Then from outside the doors . . . in the vestibule . . . you hear. "Shshpp! Shshpp! Shshpp! Shshpp! Feet moving and making a soft music all they own. "Shshpp!" "Shshpp! Shshpp! Shshpp!" Then you hear voices . . . but you ain't sure . . . they go soft. . . . "Bip! Bip! Bip! Bip!" They start to get louder. "Bip! Bip! Bip! Bip!" Louder still. "Bip! Bip! Bip! Bip!" The door fling open! The light pitch on! Pandemonium break loose, man. I tell you, costume like you never see. Everybody playing Mas and going crazy! Dame Lorraine is here! You ain't know nothing 'bout that 'cause you daddy one of them wop. No get mad. I tell he so to he face and he call me a nigger-monkey. Then we laugh. We was friend, you know. Anyway, every time we have a Dame Lorraine, me and my Dawkie come home and make a baby that night. After that, is Lent and I don't touch she again 'till after Easter come and gone. I have eight boy and one girl. What you think 'bout that. Eight boy. The girl pretty, but all girl pretty. Mine could too make a fool out of me and get anything she want. She that pretty. But you ain't see nothing like them boy on this earth . . In this world. Gods! I tell you. Gods! Skin? Black like coal and smooth like oil. Eyes? They range, I tell you. They range. One had blue. One had green. One had yellow . . . like tiger. But the first one? Oh, God. Eyes so black, they burn right through you and hold you in place. Hair like some silk magic. Newspun and blacker than mystery. Teeth? White ain't enough to describe them. He smile take everything from you. Bodies? Strong, tall and quick like cat. I walk down the street with them boy and everybody stand aside and look. Ain't nobody believe they mine, but every one of them belong to me. Every one of them born nine months to the day after the last Dame Lorraine. The spirit of Dame Lorraine in all of them.

Dum de dum de dum de dum de dee

Oh! Don't stop the carnival . . .

Dawkie, come dance with me, girl. Then we go home and make another royal baby. They all royal, you know, young man. I name them all royal. People laugh at first, but I ain't care. There was Count and Duke and Baron and Marquis and Prince and Earl and Knight, but that first one. . . . The one with the eyes like the universe. Him, I name King. King Moulineaux. Every man should have sons and God and my wife bless me eight times over. Come, Dawkie. We have to get ready. Oh, young man, only good things ever happen to me when I go to the Dame Lorraine. Come, Dawkie. You must be getting old. You can't keep up?

Dum de dum de dum de dum. . . .

DORCAS: Picton, The Duke of Iron and MacBeth the Great . . . dead! They don't make music no more. They all dead!

PICTON: For true?

DORCAS: Yes! They die long time ago. The Dame Lorraine over. It been over.

PICTON: So who making music now?

DORCAS: There's no music, Picton. Is all in you head.

PICTON: We might as well go home then.

DORCAS: Might as well.

PICTON: Good night, Ladies! Good night, young man. I know your father, you know.

(*He goes.* RENIE *comes out and stands at her door.*)

SAL: I'll come back in the morning.

DORCAS: Angela, go with him.

ANGELA: I'll stay with you.

DORCAS: Go! Come back tomorrow.

SAL: I'll take you to your place.

ANGELA: I still see those eyes.

SAL: Pity! Come on.

(*They start to go.*)

DORCAS: Angela?

(ANGELA *comes back, but she cannot kiss* DORCAS.)

ANGELA: Good night, Mother.

(ANGELA *runs out the door.*)

DORCAS: She ain't never going call me, "Moomah" again . . .

SAL: Good night, Mrs. Moulineaux.

DORCAS: Come here, young man.

(SAL *goes to* DORCAS. *She kisses him.*)

SAL: I didn't know you like Italians.

DORCAS: Don't forget, you is half-home-boy. Is that part I kissing.

SAL: Even, now . . . eh?

DORCAS: Just funning, son. Just funning. Good night.

(*He goes.*)

RENIE: Wish I had somewhere to go. I know you want to be alone with him.

DORCAS: With him. Yes, with him! Over sixty years that man see me for the first and tell me he love me. I was young . . . and scared of men, you hear? But I look at him and drop all me cards. He give me one good kiss and tell me that goin' have to hold me 'cause he goin' 'way on the boat to make money and then he coming back to marry with me . . . and I better be ready. He run off in the crowd and I had was to run after him to find out he name and tell him mine. Then I tell him, "I love you, Picton Moulineaux". Just that once. I ain't never say them word again. I ain't have to. He know. He always know. Ain't nothing change. And you ain't have to go nowhere for me to be alone with him. Where would you go? You home, girl. You home.

(RENIE *goes back inside.*)

PICTON: Dawkie! Dawkie!

DORCAS: Yes, Darling.

(*She goes into the room.*)

PICTON: I been thinking. Nothing to keep us here now. Why we don't get our ticket and go home.

DORCAS: Yes, Darling.

PICTON: You think they still have Dame Lorraine there?

DORCAS: Yes, Darling.

PICTON: Well, dance with me one more time before we go.

DORCAS: Yes, Darling.

PICTON:
    Dum de dum de dum de dum de dee
    No! Don't stop the carnival . . .
You was always the best dancer for me, girl. Dawkie?

DORCAS: Yes, Darling?

PICTON: I sorry I do this thing to you. I sorry I plant all them bad flowers in you. I ain't never want to see you cry. I beg you forgiveness. Before God, I beg you forgiveness.

DORCAS: Yes, Darling.

PICTON: Dawkie?

DORCAS: Yes, Darling?

PICTON: I too love you, girl.

DORCAS: Yes, Darling.

(*One gunshot. Then, another.*)

END

One Last Look

One Last Look premiered at the Old Reliable Theatre Tavern in New York City on 13 November 1967. The Producers were Norman "Speedy" Hartmann and Tony Preston. Arthur French directed the following cast:

EUSTACE BAYLOR	A.D. Cannon
SOPRANO	Louise Mike
CORA LEE	Mari Foreman
ADELAIDE	Gracie Carroll
FUNERAL DIRECTOR	Ensley
REVA BUTLER	Bette Howard
DONNA BUTLER	Pawnee Sills
CHARLIE BUTLER	Carl Gordon
ANNETTE BAYLOR	Barbara Clarke
APRIL BAYLOR	Denise Nicholas
STACE BAYLOR	David Downing

Thanks, Arthur French, for putting
meaning to the play and
me on the map.

Characters

THE ATTENDANT*
EUSTACE BAYLOR
THE SOPRANO
CORA LEE SIMMONS
ADELAIDE
FUNERAL DIRECTOR
REVA BUTLER
DONNA BUTLER
CHARLIE BUTLER
ANNETTE BAYLOR
APRIL BAYLOR
STACE BAYLOR

---

*Nonspeaking role inserted by Mr. Arthur French and created by Mr. Jack Landron. This person reacts to all the things that go on in the actual funeral parlor and not in memory. To me, the play seems better if this character is included. Thanks, always, To Messrs. French and Landron.

(*There is complete blackness.*)

CORA LEE: Yeah . . . this is the place. I remember from when we buried my youngest sister's old man. This is the same place.

ADELAIDE: I been to some funerals here too. Can't remember whose, but this place looks familiar. You goin' to the party . . . I mean . . . the wake . . . later on?

CORA LEE: Hungry as I am . . . I wouldn't miss it. You know, I couldn't stop and get nothin' to eat . . . had to come here straight from work . . . Reva always did make good potato salad . . . sure hope she made some for tonight . . .

ADELAIDE: Probably did . . . and I'm gonna need a drink after this. . . . Well, you ready?

CORA LEE: Yeah. . . . Come on!

(*In the darkness, an organ starts to play almost inaudibly. Slowly the lights come up. We, the audience, can make out the figure of the* SOPRANO. *She is bewigged, buxom, and all purposely, understated passion. She stands downstage center. To her left is a lectern. Behind her is a casket. The casket is a bit too ornate, perhaps, when we stop to consider that we are in a funeral parlor in the less fortunate part of Harlem . . . wherever that may be. The casket is open and though we cannot see the occupant, we know he's in there. It is flower laden. As the lights go higher, we notice the figure of* EUSTACE BAYLOR *a little behind the casket. As the* SOPRANO *starts to sing* Abide with Me, EUSTACE *smiles down on his "mortal remains."*)

(*There is a center aisle. To the left of it, in the front row, there are three vacant seats. The BUTLER FAMILY and, later, the BAYLOR FAMILY, will sit there. To the right of this same aisle are three vacant seats. The BUTLER FAMILY will occupy these. About four rows behind the BAYLOR FAMILY seats there are two vacant seats, to be occupied by* CORA LEE *and* ADELAIDE. *There is also a seat placed unobtrusively on stage to be occupied by the* SOPRANO *when she isn't singing.*)

(*Lights up.*)

CORA LEE: Lord, Lord, Lord, Honey . . . What a turnout. Seems all the old bunch is here . . . (*To the "old bunch"*) . . . Hi, Darlin', hi, Honey.

ADELAIDE: (*To the "old bunch"*) How do . . .? Hi, Sweetheart. I never knew he had so many friends.

CORA LEE: He didn't. It's just a whole lot of people can't believe he's dead . . . so they come to make sure he ain' foolin' . . .

ADELAIDE: Let's get some good seats up front so we won't miss anything.

CORA LEE: We can't go all the way up there . . . that's for the family.

ADELAIDE: Well, we can get near the family . . . besides he ain't got . . . I mean . . . he didn't have much of a family . . . (*She laughs.*)

CORA LEE: Here's some good seats right here.

ADELAIDE: Ain't you gonna look in the casket?

CORA LEE: What for? He's in there . . . ain't he?

ADELAIDE: Come on, gal. Don't be 'fraid . . . Dead people can't hurt you none . . . Let's look in . . . (*She goes up to the casket.*)

CORA LEE: Well . . . Okay. . . . (*She joins* ADELAIDE.) Well, now I believe it. The old buzzard is really dead.

CORA LEE: Well, some men got enough devil in 'em to last 'em through to hell and back. You know . . . he don't look peaceful. . . . he still look as wild as he did when he first come up here.

ADELAIDE: Yeah. . . . I sure used to have some good times with that man.

CORA LEE: Caused some happy tears to shed in this department too, Honey.

ADELAIDE: I guess he caused a whole lot of women to laugh . . .

CORA LEE: . . . and cry.

ADELAIDE: . . . and damn it, look at him. He don't look like he through yet. . . . Damn devil.

(*The* FUNERAL DIRECTOR *enters with studied solemnity, but manages a look at* CORA LEE *and* ADELAIDE *on his way to the lectern.* CORA LEE *flirts back.*)

Lord, I remember one night in thirty-four . . . him an' me come into Lazy Al's place . . . he was drunk as usual and trying to get drunker . . .

CORA LEE: Seems like he went out with a whole lot of people in thirty-four . . .

ADELAIDE: Yeah, don't it . . . anyway we come into Lazy Al's place and. . . . Oh, God . . . Here come Reva and the kids. . . . Look at that dress. . . . Lord, don't make me laugh out loud.

FUNERAL DIRECTOR: All rise. Everyone please rise.

ADELAIDE: Lord, don't make me laugh out loud.

CORA LEE: . . . never did know how to dress. . . . That's probably why he never took her out nowhere. I remember one time . . . in thirty-four, I might add . . . we all made a big party and went to one of the Lively Ladies Social Club dances and, Honey, nobody couldn't tell me I didn't look as fine as I wanted to . . . and she come in with this too small . . . too old, gold dress on. . . . Well, Honey, I thought I would . . .

(REVA *and her CHILDREN come abreast of* CORA LEE *and* ADELAIDE.)

Reva, Darlin' . . . I'm so sorry. My sympathy.

REVA: Thank you.

CORA LEE: My very deepest sympathy. Don't you lose heart now.

ADELAIDE: Yeah, the Lord will provide. You done your job, now God is gonna do his.

REVA: Thank you so much. Everybody been so nice.

(REVA, *followed by her children* DONNA *and* CHARLIE, *slowly proceed to the three seats to the left of the aisle. The* FUNERAL DIRECTOR *offers them his sympathy.*)

CORA LEE: (*To* REVA *from her seat three rows behind.*) If you need anything . . . anything . . . you remember Cora Lee Simmons is standing by. I brought my smelling salts for when you faint . . .

ADELAIDE: Me, too!

REVA: Everybody just been so nice . . . (*Sits*)

ADELAIDE: Yes, you poor thing. (*To* CORA LEE) . . . poor thing is right. She fightin' that dress, ain't she?

FUNERAL DIRECTOR: Be seated please.

(*All sit.*)

FUNERAL DIRECTOR: We gather this evening to pay our last respects to a man . . . who from now on will be with us only in our hearts. . . . Our departed brother, Eustace Baylor. The family has requested that his favorite hymn . . .

ADELAIDE: Hah!

FUNERAL DIRECTOR: . . . "Nearer My God To Thee," be sung . . .

SOPRANO: (*Rises from her chair and stands over the BUTLER FAMILY, and sings.*) "Nearer My God To Thee. . . ." (*etc.*)

CORA LEE: Hypocrite. He never even knew what the inside of a church looked like much less had a favorite hymn. . . . Remember his old saying, "What I don't do today, I ain't gonna do tomorrow . . .?"

ADELAIDE: Yeah. . . . Lord, look at them kids. You'd think they'd have a little respect for the dead. That boy's head's so nappy . . . you could get lost in it . . .

CORA LEE: Must be one of them hundred twenty fifth-street Africans . . .

ADELAIDE: He ain't nothing 'cept dirty. His shirt's dirty. His shoes' dirty. . . . He's dirty. . . . He sure didn't take after his father. Eustace always was clean . . . even if he was a dirty dog. . . . The gal ain't much better. She like her momma. . . . They look frowsy. . . . How they can come in . . .

CORA LEE: Sweet Jesus. . . . Look who come in. . . .

ADELAIDE: Who? Who? Oh, no . . . it's her. What's his wife doing here. . . . His son and daughter too . . .?

CORA LEE: Talk about nerve . . .

ADELAIDE: Got to hand it to the little monkey-chaser. . . . She still look good . . . under all that make-up.

CORA LEE: Where they gonna sit? Jesus wept and father crept, they walkin' up the aisle. Talk about nerve . . . told you these was good seats. I wouldn't've missed this for the world. . . . Lord! Lord! Lord!

ADELAIDE: (*As the BAYLOR FAMILY comes abreast.*) Hi, Annette. You don't remember me, do you?

ANNETTE: (*All ice*) I know you.

CORA LEE: You got my deepest sympathy . . . Annette.

ANNETTE: (*Icier*) Really?

CORA LEE: Your kids sure grew up . . .

STACE: There was nothing better to do in the last thirty some-odd years.

APRIL: . . . so like "Topsy", we "just growed." Come on, Mother . . . this is your idea. . . . Let's get it over with.

(*The BAYLORS start to walk toward the first row.*)

ADELAIDE: Damn, dirty West Indians. . . . Sure hope they don't come to the wake and spoil everybody's fun . . .

ADELAIDE: (*Standing over REVA.*) Will you please get up.

REVA: (*Startled*) What . . .?

CHARLIE: You can't talk to my mother like that . . .

STACE: (*Restraining* CHARLIE) The front row is reserved for the wife and children. . . . Inasmuch as he fathered us and sired you . . . you can stay . . . however . . . your mother . . .

DONNA: Ma, you sit right where you are. . . . You the one had to put up with all the crap . . .

REVA: I'll move. I don't want no trouble. I'll sit in the front row on the other side . . . (*Rises and starts over.*)

ANNETTE: I think that's wisest.

REVA: Come on y'all.

CHARLIE: (*Purposely bumping into* STACE.) . . . Shi . . .

STACE: You mustn't bump into me again, half-brother. We must respect that thing lying there . . .

APRIL: Come on, Stace. Sit down.

STACE: (*To* CHARLIE) Go to your mother.

CHARLIE: You ain't shit . . .

STACE: Thank you so much . . . and if that's your way of telling me that you are . . . I understand and agree . . .

ANNETTE AND APRIL: Stace . . . Sit down . . .

REVA AND DONNA: Charlie . . . come on over here . . . sit down . . .

ADELAIDE: Talk about nerve . . . now, that's nerve.

CORA LEE: Yeah, that's nerve. I told you these was good seats. I sure wouldn't't've missed this . . .

FUNERAL DIRECTOR: Friends, I have been asked to be brief because Eustace Baylor's stay on this Earth was brief. Eustace was almost sixty but he had lived so much . . . so fast . . . and probably never lived at all . . . but he had so much life left that it seemed, to those who knew and possibly loved him . . . that he was here all too briefly . . . (*Freeze*)

DONNA: Not briefly enough. (*Rises and approaches the casket.*) Oh, Daddy, why'd you have to go to bed with my momma? Why couldn't you stay at home with your wife where you belonged? Why couldn't you let me be your wife's daughter so I could've got to be something? Why did you force me to be this woman's daughter so that I had to love her . . . and be loyal to her . . . and not get away from her? Daddy, why am

I thirty-four years old ... with nine kids and looking like I was fifty. ... Can you tell me anything?

EUSTACE: Questions. So many questions all at once, Little Lady ...

DONNA: I have to know. All I ever did was wonder ... now I have to know.

EUSTACE: Missy, I can't give you the answers now ... but I know you mustn't hate me. Don't hate me now. I got no way of fighting that now. I did my best for you and ... I loved you ...

DONNA: ... and I loved you, Daddy ... but you kept me down. Every boy. ... Every man I ever met was you, Daddy. Just you all over again. I loved you so much that I had to love them. ... Guess it's my lot to go through life falling for no-good men ... or men who ain't no good for me ...

EUSTACE: It's terrible to be dead. There's no feeling. I can't even miss the good times we had together. Nights when I'd come home sick ...

DONNA: Oh, Daddy, not now. Be honest. You're so used to lying ... you lying in your coffin ...

EUSTACE: Hah! You always was one for the joke. I sure am lying in my coffin. Yeah ... nights I'd come home drunk and happy and you'd take my shoes off and sing to me ... or when I wasn't happy ... you'd soothe me and tell me I was the only man in the whole, wide world for you ... oh, good times.

DONNA: Good times ...

EUSTACE: I still don't know if there's a God but, if there is, I sure wish He'd let me feel myself missing those good times ...

DONNA: I feel enough for both of us, Daddy. ... Good-bye. I loved you so. Why'd you have to be my daddy. You should've been somebody else. God! If you was just somebody else ... another man ... I could have loved you better. I know how to love other men ... we could have had oh ... a something. Good-bye ... good-bye ... (Sits)

FUNERAL DIRECTOR: It seems that he was here long enough to say hello and that's all. It is, for me, a doubly sad occasion because Eustace and I were children together in Richmond. We were friends. We went to school together and, sometimes, we didn't go to school together. ... We came north to this city together. ... Now, here he lies as I eulogize ... (Pleased with himself) We all knew Eustace. We all knew him as a man with faults. Major in the eyes of some ... minor to others ... but one quality he did have was the unfailing ability to not pull punches. (Freeze)

APRIL: You were honest. (*Rises*) You made no secret of your brutal, crippling honesty. Remember how honest you were when I was fifteen? Remember telling me that I should marry somebody . . . anybody . . . so you wouldn't have to support me anymore?

EUSTACE: Yes, I remember . . . and I had two good reasons.

APRIL: You certainly did. One was a fifth . . . the other a quart.

EUSTACE: You never did understand me.

APRIL: Never understood . . . you? Why, if it weren't for my brother constantly drumming it into my head that you were my father, I could have gone safely through my life never even knowing you.

EUSTACE: I had two families to support. You and your brother and your mother. You didn't need me. Who did Charlie and Donna have . . . Reva?

APRIL: Yes . . . and they had you!

EUSTACE: They needed me.

APRIL: No. You needed them. They didn't need you. Did Donna need you to encourage her to be a crumpled piece of womanhood at thirty-four? And look at Charlie . . . about to die from wine at thirty-three. He and I are the same age and look at him . . . burned away. . . . They didn't need the particular brand of help you dispense . . .

EUSTACE: They'd've never made out at all if I'd left them with Reva. . . . Look at her. She ain't smart and she ain't pretty. She loved me, though. I was all she could get and she loved me. And she needed me. . . . Those kids needed me.

APRIL: I needed you . . . to tell me I was Daddy's girl . . . to sneak into the bathroom and cry when you saw me as I put on my first grown-up clothes . . . to miss me on my wedding night after placing me in the love and care of my husband. Did Donna need you for that? Did you give her to a man? Or did you turn your head away as she went to bed with just . . . man after man . . . after man . . . ?

EUSTACE: You had your mother.

APRIL: . . . and she was too busy being a father to be a mother . . . too busy doing your job . . . to do hers . . .

EUSTACE: She should have realized you needed a father and tried to do something about it . . .

APRIL: She did . . . and don't you criticize my mother. She tried to get fathers for us. She tried to get someone to do your job for you, but we

---

wouldn't accept it. We wanted our own father and not some conveniently manufactured article. We wanted you to realize the duty. You could have come home and Stace and I would've forgiven you. . . . Mother might have never . . . but we would have . . .

EUSTACE: Well, your mother raised you too high above me . . . just like herself. I sent you toys at Christmas . . . and you never even thanked me. You were older than the toys. You seemed to just tolerate the toys as you tolerated me . . . and I couldn't stand being tolerated. I remember my own daddy saying once, "Never be tolerated. That's what colored folks do with roaches . . . they tolerate them . . . and if you want to be on the same level with roaches. . . ."

APRIL: I didn't tolerate the toys. I loathed them because I loathed Christmas. Christmas was a time for daddies to dress up like Santa Claus and try to fool their kids. Where were you? Christmas is merely the birthday celebration of a dead Jew. When my birthdays came around, where were you? I remember asking once on one of my birthdays . . . A "no-toy-from-Daddy" birthday . . . "Doesn't Daddy love me? Why doesn't he at least come by and let me know that he'll always remember this day because it's the day I came to him . . .?" I'll bet you never forgot Donna's birthday . . .

EUSTACE: I can't say that I feel sorrow for what I did or didn't do for you . . . I want to but, it's too late . . . for anything and everything . . .

APRIL: Yes, you were honest to everyone except yourself. Good-bye. . . . I don't know whether or not we shall meet again, but I sincerely hope not because I can never again give you the chance to hurt me. . . . It is too late for everything . . . too late for me to even forgive you . . . (Sits)

FUNERAL DIRECTOR: Some of us knew him as a sinner . . . yet, here was a man who talked to God . . .

CORA LEE AND ADELAIDE: Amen! Yes, Lord!

FUNERAL DIRECTOR: A man who talked to God on his own terms . . . A man who made God sit up and notice him . . .

CORA LEE AND ADELAIDE: Yes, God! Do, Lord!

FUNERAL DIRECTOR: When we were kids, he'd sit up on the roof in Richmond and talk to God.

CORA LEE: Amen!

FUNERAL DIRECTOR: I used to hear him talking to God so deeply that more than once, I could swear I heard God answer him.

ADELAIDE: Amen. . . . Oh, Sweet Jesus, Amen! Amen!

CORA LEE: Forgive him, Lord!

REVA: Oh, God, help me. . . . He gone My man gone! Help me.

CORA LEE: (*Rushing to* REVA . . . ADELAIDE *in hot pursuit.*) Give her some air. Let me fan her . . . Let me fan her . . .

ADELAIDE: Let me give her some smelling salts . . .

CORA LEE: Dammit! I forgot I got some too . . .

ADELAIDE: (*To* CORA LEE) Too late, honey. (*To* REVA) Here, Child. . . . A whiff of this will do you good.

CORA LEE: Well, at least let me fan her . . .

DONNA: If you don't mind, I'll take care of her . . .

CORA LEE AND ADELAIDE: 'Scuse me . . . Well! (*Retreating to their seats.*)

STACE: (*To the* FUNERAL DIRECTOR) Would you please get on with it.

FUNERAL DIRECTOR: Eustace Baylor was a man who never asked for anything . . . (*Freeze*)

CHARLIE: That's true (*Rises*) You ain't never asked me for a thing. You ain't never asked me for love. . . . You ain't never asked me for hate . . .

EUSTACE: Did you want that?

CHARLIE: I wanted something . . . some feeling . . . anything. I am a person.

EUSTACE: I gave you all I could. I gave you clothes . . . I gave you food. I kept people from bothering you . . . even after I found out about you . . .

CHARLIE: I swore up and down then . . . I swear now . . . that was the only time . . . THE ONLY TIME.

EUSTACE: One time too many . . .

CHARLIE: I was so young . . .

EUSTACE: Sixteen . . .

CHARLIE: Was that too old to be forgiven. I wasn't too old to beg for it. You never understood or tried to understand me. You accused me from the start. "Put down that damn fiddle." "Only little girls play the fiddle." I had music all inside of me and you sucked it all out.

EUSTACE: You showed me what you had in you when you was sixteen . . . and it wasn't me that did the sucking . . .

CHARLIE: It's the only thing I ever wanted from you . . . just the chance to make music. A chance to come off of that block. . . . A chance to live clean like Stace and April . . .

EUSTACE: You ain't Stace . . .

CHARLIE: Well, if you taking credit for him, you got to take credit for me. You got just as much in me as you got in him.

EUSTACE: We only got your ma's word for that.

CHARLIE: Oh, I'm yours all right. You can go to hell and come back three times and that's still gonna be a fact.

EUSTACE: Stace is a man!

CHARLIE: We don't even have his word for that but, you're right . . . He is whole. I envy him for that . . . but, I used to be a man . . .

EUSTACE: As long as you know what you are now . . .

CHARLIE: I know what I am. I'm a sponge. I've soaked up all the wetness and rottenness of you . . . and I've become you. I've even outdone you. I've been drunk for the last seventeen years and I don't figure to let up. I'm gonna kick in soon and the only thing that bothers me about dying is that maybe all that crap about there being a heaven and a hell is true. If it is, I know I'll be going to hell and you'll be there already. The hell of it would be to be hated by my daddy all through hell and not being able to get away from it. Imagine . . . having no way out from you. Come to think of it, the hell is not where you are. In a way, it's where I am. I've had hell all my life and always will. You're gonna hate me from the grave. Even in whatever short time I got left, I ain't gonna know what peace is. . . . You left here hating and not forgiving me.

EUSTACE: I don't hate you. I never hated you. To say I hated you means that once I had to love you. Why waste all that good, hot feeling on whatever it is you are. I don't have any feeling for you.

CHARLIE: Oh, God . . .

EUSTACE: . . . truth of the matter is, I hate myself for having been responsible . . . no . . . not responsible . . . to blame for your being here . . .

CHARLIE: No. . . . No. . . . Please, Daddy . . . hate me. Let me have that if nothing else. . . . Let me have something from you. . . . Don't leave me with nothing.

EUSTACE: If I could have only seen into the future . . . I would have castrated myself before I sired a freak boy.

CHARLIE: No more, please. Let me say good-bye to you. . . . You know, I remember once I called you, "Daddy" and you slapped me right in the mouth. My lip bled for five minutes and my heart's been bleeding ever since . . . but, I have the perfect replacement for all that blood I lost . . . (*Produces a bottle of cheap wine.*) Here's to you, Daddy. (*He takes a swallow.*) Now, come on . . . slap me again . . . again . . . harder . . . harder . . . Now, feel these tears . . . They're for you and you can't stop me from crying for you . . . because you're dead . . . (*Collapses in his seat.*)

FUNERAL DIRECTOR: He's dead but, let us think of death as a sleep. A sleep from which somewhere . . . someday we will awaken. We pray that God will watch over our sleeping brother, Eustace Baylor, until he can awaken to restart his life. . . . A life in which, possibly, all the mistakes of his last life will be rectified. . . . and after all, . . . what is an awakening? No more than a new day to open our eyes and hope with all our hearts we can do better than yesterday.

STACE: No! We can't go through it again . . . (*Rises*) That kind of tomorrow is just a yesterday all over again . . . and, Father, you are not worth going through a yesterday twice, are you?

EUSTACE: Eustace . . . Little Eustace . . .

STACE: Little Eustace is as dead as you are. . . . I call myself Stace.

EUSTACE: You grew up to look just like your momma's daddy.

STACE: I deem that a compliment . . . So would he, were he here. Fortunately or unfortunately, you'll never be able to tell him that, will you?

EUSTACE: You must hate me.

STACE: No.

EUSTACE: Well, you can't have any love for me . . .

STACE: You're right there . . .

EUSTACE: Do you feel anything for me?

STACE: Let me say this. Your blood flows in me. I can't do anything about it . . . nor do I complain. . . . In fact, in my particular society, I say as little about it as possible. . . . But all through my life, the family . . . my family . . . has made it clear . . . at every possible opportunity . . . that I was a bit tainted because of your black, southern blood in me . . .

EUSTACE: My blood was just as good as the blood of any God-damned monkey-chaser.

STACE: Let's debate that when we meet again . . .

EUSTACE: After all . . . southerners are just West Indians that didn't stop off . . .

STACE: With one difference . . . Pride. The West Indian has always or damned near always had it . . . The southerner has just begun to acquire it in large doses . . . You, personally, never had it.

EUSTACE: Damned if you didn't come out talking like your ma's daddy.

STACE: That, too, is a compliment. Even if what you have to say is garbled . . . it's better to say something than to sit on the porch and rock away your troubles . . . and, baby, let's face it . . . that's how I remember your daddy . . . just a-sittin' on the verandah . . . rockin' and a-rockin' and sayin', "I don' wan' me no trouble." My grandfather was a fool but he was a fighter. Your father was never even a contender . . . and you were only a flyweight. You let that old man beat you out of what you had won from him. I just have no feeling for you because . . . though I don't mind winners or losers . . . I have nothing for those who never even try to go the distance.

EUSTACE: . . . and that's me . . . ?

STACE: Check! Now, about the love/hate thing. It's impossible for me to love you because I hate the things you've done . . . and then again, hate is a rather splendid emotion. It's worthy only of kings, emperors, or presidents. Do you honestly consider yourself fit to travel in such illustrious and lofty company? Besides, I don't really know you, do I? You can't spend all that magnificent venom on a stranger now, can you?

EUSTACE: A true snake strikes anything he sees.

STACE: God, in His infinite wisdom, is not perfect and I can't help it if he made the snake indiscriminate. Snakes should only strike down the things that mean them harm. It's the way . . . the only way to get along. It's the way I get along.

EUSTACE: Are you a snake?

STACE: Only to those I've struck down. What do you think I am?

EUSTACE: Something I think I'm sorry I had a hand in . . .

STACE: Your knowledge of anatomy mistifies me a bit, but I'll accept that. . . . And now, I'll tell you what I think you are. You are my "raison d'etre". . . . My reason for being. . . . My motivation. I just knew whatever I was going to be, I had to overcome you. You know, when we had to stay those two weeks with you in the summers . . . and you would take us, your two legitimate children and your two illegitimate children . . . you would take the four of us around to whatever whore you were cheating on your mistress with that year . . .? Well, whenever we would meet your latest chit, remember how you used to say . . . with your chest swelled with pride over showing off your little whelps . . . "Kids, meet your newest mother"? Remember that? Well, you hurt all four of us, sir. You hurt four children and insulted two women who, for all your filth, never said an unkind word against you. I said then, "I have to overcome this. And Charles. . . . Poor, defeated Charlie. Poor, once-beautiful and deep Charlie. You saw him rush to me in his innocence and kiss me full on my mouth. You tuned him out without asking why . . . without yelling at him . . . without beating him. That boy, who has become just another wino, kissed me in gratitude because I, his half-brother . . . not his father, not his mother, but his half-brother, had saved up his money and bought him a violin. You know what he said to me? He said "You have given my soul a way to escape. You have given me a beautiful freedom. I promise you that every glorious note I shall play, will be in payment for what you have done for me. I shall make my life a dedication to you." He kissed me and said, "I know no other way, Brother. I am too happy." He turned away to let those big, beautiful tears splash over the instrument . . . never dreaming that you were lurking in the shadows . . . making evil out of all that was beauty . . .

And later, when he came to tell that you had smashed the violin, he cried and said the thing that hurt him most was that you just smashed it on the wall and not over his head. He said you didn't even care enough for that.

EUSTACE: Course I didn't care. What's left in life when your son is a . . .

STACE: Your son was a beautiful happening . . . because in spite of you and that old bitch being fanned by those two harpies . . . something grand was about to happen. A fine rose was about to bloom despite a union of the worst of the low-grade fertilizers. And I, who stood mute when he first thanked me with his kiss, leading you to think that I disapproved, now found a way to show him that I loved him. I took him to my room and we lay side by side . . . his head cradled in my arms . . . and we . . . cried. We made up for the lost years and the difference in mothers. We were two small brothers whose father had just beaten the hell out of them . . . and we were hurt. I wonder what you would have said if you had come in and witnessed that scene. . . . "Anyhoo," I said to myself again, "I have to overcome this man." And though I promised Charlie I'd get him another "fiddle," I never did. I grew away from him because all I had my mind on was growing away from you . . . and I've made it. I am in and don't let anyone tell you I'm not and, Father, I owe it all to you. Whatever my good mother did for me to make me a success, she could only supply the wherewithal . . . but, Daddy, you supplied the drive. Mother always kept a picture of you and I would sneak into her room to look at it and say, "That's a fine sone you're not raising there, Mr. Baylor. He'll be a credit to you one day." And it's true. I can safely say, Daddy, you made me what I am today. I hope you're satisfied. 'Bye now . . . you lousy bastard . . . (*Sits*)

EUSTACE: Oh, God. Let me have some feeling. I have to feel something. Is the sould dead too? They always said the soul never died . . . That the sould was the feeling place. Why can't I have some feeling?

FUNERAL DIRECTOR: Some say Eustace Baylor was a man without feeling . . . a man without a soul. . . . Well, I don't know about that. I do know that he was a man who lacked ability to communicate. . . . A man who always should have said things but couldn't or wouldn't . . . and didn't. Whatever his faults, and he may have had many, we have to forgive him now . . . because we are only mortal. Only God should hold any grudge now and I expect Eustace is finding out right now whether or not He does.

REVA: Now, what can I do? You gone . . . and I'm here . . . by myself . . .

EUSTACE: You got the kids . . .

REVA: What kids? Donna? Charlie? Donna got so many kids of her own. I tell her she ain't smart workin' the streets without her tubes tied up but, she say it ain't Godly. . . . She can't help me 'cause she out trying to find somebody to take of her and her'n . . . and Charlie? Forget it. He's gonna die soon. It's sittin' all over him.

EUSTACE: You'll make out.

REVA: How . . . on my looks? If I tred to get by on my looks, I'd be on my way to the poorhouse from this funeral. Besides, I don't mean that.

EUSTACE: Well, if that's all you want, you can get that from any man or horse for that matter.

REVA: You goin' to your grave not knowin' me. Thinkin' that I was so crazy in love with you that that was the reason I put up with all the hurtin' that you put on me. Well, I gotta tell you the truth. I can't let you lay there forever feelin' smug. I gotta tell you that I never loved you. I only needed somebody.

EUSTACE: Me!

REVA: Somebody! Anybody! I was hopin' I would die before I met you. . . . There was only my folks tellin' me I was big . . . dumb . . . clumsy . . . stupid. . . . Ugly!

EUSTACE: You hold yourself lightly.

REVA: They held me . . . you and them . . . held me lightly. Me . . . with all that lovely feelin' inside of me and nobody willin' to take it. Me . . . who wanted to read books and go to plays and talk about things goin' on in the world. Nobody willin' to look inside me. Anyway, you know what the happies' moment in my life was?

EUSTACE: I can guess.

REVA: No . . . you can't. It wasn't any one time you and I was in bed or anything like that. It was the day you finally come to me and said, "I lef' Annette . . . once and for all." I called up my folks and told them I had won me a man away from a pretty woman . . . a pretty, light skinned, monkey woman too. Firs' time in my life I ever felt like a woman.

EUSTACE: I didn't know you had all that stored up in you, Reva.

REVA: 'Course you didn't. Nobody blaming you for bein' like the rest of the people. When other broads would see me walkin' down the street, they would wonder what it was I had to take a good lookin' man like you away from a fine lookin' West Indian broad like that. For the first time, I could walk down the block with my head up and a smile on my face . . . one of them mysterious smiles that women smile when they know somethin' nobody else knows. . . . People used to laugh at me and I know it . . . but soon they stopped and started wonderin' what there was to me . . . so I didn't mind you runnin' around with all them other women 'cause you came back home at night. Tell you the truth, sometimes I would start wonderin' why you kept comin' back home. Then, one day, I figured out that I was like one of them safety zones they got in the street where no cars supposed to bother you. I was just somebody that you could use as an excuse so you wouldn't have to get more mixed up with more women than you already was. . . . But all that's over with. I ain' gonna be able to hold up my head no more. . . . I'm gettin' old. You helped as much as Mother Nature with that. And I just ain't gonna matter to nobody soon. . . . I'll be just another misfit. There's new things and new kinds of people . . . I ain't gonna fit in.

EUSTACE: You're right there . . . but if it's true for you. . . . It was true for me. Both of us was yesterday's children. Neither one of us could do anything about the new times heading our way.

REVA: But you out of it now . . . And I got to face it by myself. . . . All by myself. When I think of all the misery that's gonna come my way . . . I could scream . . . I have to scream . . . Ain't nothin' else I can do . . . (*Collapsing in her seat, she screams back to reality.*)

CORA LEE: Oh, God. Poor thing . . . I'm comin'. (*Rushes to* REVA'*s side.*)

ADELAIDE: (*In hot pursuit of* CORA LEE.) Help her, Lord, help her.

CORA LEE: Move out the way, Adelaide. I got here first this time.

ADELAIDE: (*Bewildered, and crossing over to* ANNETTE.) Oh, it's such a sad time. Nothin' anybody can do about it. You don't feel faint or anything, do you?

ANNETTE: Really!

ADELAIDE: I thought not but, in case you do, I got some smelling salts and I'd be happy to do anything.

ANNETTE: No!

APRIL: Thank you! No!

(ADELAIDE *and a triumphant* CORA LEE *return to their seats.*)

STACE: You know, if I were entertaining thoughts of becoming an actor's agent, this is where I would come for the major portion of my clientele. Some of the better performances are put on at funerals. The pity of it is that there are so few agents at these affairs.

APRIL: Well, some people need this kind of drama. It's the only way some people can show there false feelings.

ANNETTE: . . . and their true feelings.

FUNERAL DIRECTOR: To conclude . . . I should like to ask the Lord on behalf of my sleeping friend to protect his soul and forgive him his sons. This is something I know he would never do . . . and it's probably a clue why he had to die, as he, with his last words described it, "an unhappy man." Let us pray.

SOPRANO: (*Rises, stands at a point midway of both the families and sings.*) "When I come to the end of my journey" . . . etc.

(FUNERAL DIRECTOR *comes to help* REVA *up to view the remains. . . . She screams and almost faints.* CORA LEE *and* ADELAIDE *rush to her, offering adlib ministrations.* DONNA *looks at the corpse, smiles, and exits.* CHARLIE *goes to the casket, kisses the corpse, and, out of sight of the other mourners, places therein his wine bottle.* STACE *and* APRIL *rise—both ignore the casket.*)

APRIL: Come on, Mother.

ANNETTE: I'll be out in a moment. Leave me for a while.

STACE: Oh, come on, Mother. Why do you want to sit here? I would have thought you had enough of this circus by now.

ANNETTE: The reason for all my actions in the last thirty-eight years of my life is lying there and I have to ask myself whether or not it's all been worth it. Part of the question is answered when I look at the two of you. . . . The other part, I have to find out for myself. . . . Please now, I will be out in a few moments.

APRIL: Come on, Stace.

STACE: We'll wait outside.

ANNETTE: Thank you.

STACE: No, Mother. Thank you.

APRIL: . . . for everything . . .

(STACE *and* APRIL *start out.*)

CORA LEE: (*Rushing in with* ADELAIDE.) Lord, we forgot about you all . . .

ADELAIDE: We came back to see if you needed anything . . .

STACE: My mother is a Rock of Gibraltar, but my sister and I could use your assistance. . . . Ladies, will you escort us?

ADELAIDE: Be glad to do anything we can. You know, we knew your father.

CORA LEE: Oh, yes. Fine man. Fine man.

STACE: So I understand.

CORA LEE: Ain't your momma coming out, Honey?

APRIL: Not just yet. Come!

(APRIL *and* STACE *steer them out. The* SOPRANO *exits.* ANNETTE *rises . . . goes to the coffin and brushes her fingers along the "face" of her dead husband.*)

ANNETTE: Well, I'm here.

EUSTACE: I knew you would be. You still look good. In fact, you look like a young girl about to be married.

ANNETTE: Still the charmer with words? I'm old!

EUSTACE: You'll never be old . . . "Netta."

ANNETTE: "Netta." It's been years. Nobody has called me that in years.

EUSTACE: Nobody?

ANNETTE: Nobody! I wouldn't let them.

EUSTACE: Netta, I'm sorry.

ANNETTE: Oh, Eustace. Now you're sorry. Why couldn't you have been sorry before. I've had nobody in all these years.

EUSTACE: Come on, now. You've had some boyfriends . . .

ANNETTE: Little flashes. Small flames. Never again that someone that lit up my life. Someone like you happens to a woman once and that's all. And maybe that's good. Women aren't strong enough to take more than one of you in a lifetime. We don't deserve that much punishment.

EUSTACE: And you . . . My whole downward road was paved with love for you . . . like a fever . . . a fever for which I had no cure . . .

ANNETTE: The cure was coming home to me.

EUSTACE: I was never good enough. Your father made that clear enough. If you weren't already pregnant, we would have never been married.

ANNETTE: You should have listened to your own heart and not to my father.

EUSTACE: You should have pleaded my case.

ANNETTE: What for? I had a husband to do any pleading for me. I was prepared to do nothing but love my husband. That's all I had to do. I had to provide him with all the comforts and a home with love in it.

EUSTACE: Like a good old-fashioned West Indian girl?

ANNETTE: Yes. That will bother you to the end of time. I didn't fall in love with a Southerner. I didn't fall for a West Indian. I thought I married someone who had chosen to be just a man. That's all I ever wanted.

EUSTACE: You didn't know what you wanted then. You were only seventeen.

ANNETTE: I knew I wanted you . . . and if I was unpolished in anything else, I was young enough to be taught. Any man who can't get what he wants and needs from a seventeen-year-old girl, is not a man . . . he's just impatient.

EUSTACE: There you go again . . . putting yourself above me.

ANNETTE: It only seems so because you put yourself beneath me. Even now. You're a spectre now . . . can't you get over the spectre of my father . . .

EUSTACE: I can't help that. It was the first time a colored man had told me that I wasn't good enough for his daughter. I got to thinking that I was going to go through the whole of my life being just no good in the eyes of everybody . . . and a man don't deserve that. He's got to be good enough for somebody. That was buzzing all inside my head the night I raped you. We could have had everything nice and proper if only he hadn't rejected me. I'll bet he would have preferred you to live common-law with any West Indian man than to be married to me . . . but I loved you . . .

ANNETTE: Thank God that I loved you or he might have made me do just that. . . . My father was a fool and you should have told him so . . . but, he believed in himself as a man. I know now that I was just as wrong not to have had a stronger belief in you . . . not to trust you further . . . but I was young . . . so young . . . I had known you as a wild, stormy thing. I used to pitch myself into cold baths because I had seen you walk down the street. Once I thought I would kill myself because you walked near me and never touched me. I tried to throw myself into your path, but always you missed touching me. I would think to myself, "To have him, just isn't enough. If I could just rip him open and crawl inside and sew him up around me . . ." I don't think that would have been close enough. God, I wanted to be a woman and you forced me to be a lady. And for the record, you never raped me. I raped you. I planned that. I fanned every flame that burned in you that night. You couldn't have gotten away even if I wanted to let you. Even I wasn't in control of what I felt for you. But, my father cowed you . . . and my wild, turbulent idol came crashing to the ground and lay, like so many fleshy pieces, at my feet. I just couldn't go on believing in you. I was young. I was in love. . . . And I was hurt.

EUSTACE: I want another chance.

ANNETTE: It's done . . .

EUSTACE: I have to have another chance. You mean I walked through this life and didn't prove a thing.

ANNETTE: You left your mark . . . on many people . . .

EUSTACE: But that means that I never even walked through life. It means that I only slithered below life . . . taking little nips out of the legs of people.

ANNETTE: To some people the bites were fatal. Others never let it get them down. But, you still left your mark even if you never proved anything to yourself. People will know you were here . . . and that's what counts.

EUSTACE: Trying to prove something to other people is just one gigantic way of saying, "I told you so." . . . and life is too short to say, "I told you so" every day of it. If I had another chance, I'd surely go after the things that I wanted and keep the things that were mine.

ANNETTE: All that sacrifice. All to show you. All to tell you, "I told you so." I told myself it was all for the kids. Everything was "the kids" . . . "the kids" . . . "the kids." The "I-told-you-so's" from my family . . . the settlements for serenity in place of your savage love. It wasn't for the kids at all. . . . It was all to show you. . . . My father left his mark on me. . . . I'm his child . . . I could have . . . should have begged you to come back to me. . . . I could have had some life . . .

EUSTACE: We're no different from the rest of the people who live on this Earth. . . . Both of us wishing, now, when it's too late, that we had it to do over. . . . Nobody ever sees things right until they're like us . . . either too old . . . or dead . . .

ANNETTE: It's been worth it. You must know that. I can say that to you and then go out of here and put on the mask for the crowd out there. . . . If all I had was just one year with you, it was worth it . . . and I had four years. Four years in which every tear I shed was an extreme pleasure . . . I thank you for them.

EUSTACE: And I, you!

ANNETTE: Good-bye! (*She turns and walks up the center aisle.*)

EUSTACE: Oh, Netta . . . (*She stops*) Good-bye!

(ANNETTE *continues until she's off.*)

(*At this point, the* SOPRANO, *through with her business for the night, comes out and walks up the aisle, humming a tune to herself. As she passes* EUSTACE, *he gives her an approving leer, a possible wink, and the lights go out.*)

END

Mirage

Characters

WOMAN
MAN

(*A female burglar enters an apartment via its fire escape window and ransacks the place, looking for small and portable items. Hearing keys at the door, she hides in a closet. A man enters, sees the condition of the place, and picks up the phone.*)

MAN: Hello, Police? I've been robbed. Come over! I've been robbed. What do you mean, "calm down!"? I've been robbed! No! No! My apartment. Okay! Okay! Burglarized, then. What difference does it make? My address is two twenty . . . What? I have to come over there? Don't you even want to dust for fingerprints or whatever it is you do? Hello? Hello? Well, I'll be damned!

WOMAN: Okay, Mack. Freeze!

MAN: I'll be damned!

WOMAN: Probably . . . if you don't get those hands up, Bosco!

MAN: But . . . you're a woman.

WOMAN: Wanna make something of it, Mandrake?

MAN: Women don't rob . . . er . . . burgle apartments.

WOMAN: It's a new day, Buster!

MAN: I don't believe this!

WOMAN: (*Motioning with a gun.*) Believe this, Jocko!

MAN: I'll not be intimidated by a woman.

WOMAN: (*Indicating gun.*) Then be intimidated by this, Buddy.

MAN: But . . . I'm a man.

WOMAN: Does that necessarily mean you have to be stupid, Booby?

MAN: What is it you want? I don't have much.

WOMAN: Not from where I'm standing, Lover.

MAN: I have a television. Take it and get out!

WOMAN: Nineteen inches? You're bigger than that, I'll bet, Pet. Ain't you got no "State of the Art" stuff, MacDuff?

MAN: No!

WOMAN: You know, I don't like your tone or your 'tude. Same old double standard shit, again. 'Cause I'm a woman, you ain't scared enough, right? You think I won't really use this. (*She puts gun to his head.*) Hah! Ready to pee in your pants now? Betcha you're thinking, "This bitch is really gonna kill me. If I had that gun, I'd show her a thing or three." eh, Butch?

MAN: Please. This has gone far enough. Please go and I won't say anything.

WOMAN: Shut up, Louie!

(*She whacks him with the gun. He sprawls.*)

WOMAN: Galls you, don't it, Laddie Bucko. A fine broth of boy like you being laid low by a mere slip of a lass, Ass

MAN: Don't . . .

WOMAN: Don't hurt you? Are you begging this "woman" for mercy, Percy?

MAN: Please . . .

WOMAN: Say your Act of Contrition, Dude.

MAN: No! Please . . . listen . . .

WOMAN: Strip, Pip!

MAN: What?

WOMAN: Strip! Outta the duds! Off mit der hosen, Rosen!

MAN: I beg your pardon . . .

WOMAN: I beg your hardon. Didn't think I was going to pass this up, did you, Liebling?

MAN: But this is . . .

WOMAN: Right, Termite! A little trick we learned from you guys. It's called Rape, Ape!

MAN: But, I can't . . .

WOMAN: It's either that or you get it right where the Monogahela and the Allegheny meet to form the Ohio, Chico!

MAN: Pittsburgh?

WOMAN: Right in the mills, Baby Doll! See how you like it when the shoe's on the other foot. Take it off! Take it all off, Orloff!

(*She threatens to whack him again. He strips down to his skivvies as she hums* "The Stripper.")

WOMAN: Man. You ain't half bad, Dad. Sorry I gotta tie your hands. Don't want you trying no Boy Scout shit to ruin my fun. 'Sides, you won't be needing your hands. Won't gag you though. You're gonna need your mouth. If you get my drift. Plus . . . I want you to tell me you love what I'm doing and how I'm the best and all that . . . Don't tell me I ain't an incurable romantic! See? I even turn the lights out for some atmosphere. Now, Sport, to work! Ooh . . . there's more to you than meats the eye. Get it? More to you than M-E-A-T-S the eye. Get to it, Macho-Man! Mama let you live a little longer, you do it right.

(*Grunts, groans, and stuff. The gun goes off. The lights come on.*)

MAN: Wow! What a fuckin' turn-on! Your dad told me I'd not ever regret the day I married you.

WOMAN: Your dad told me the same thing. What've you planned for tomorrow?

MAN: And spoil the surprise?

BLACKOUT

Tea on Inauguration Day

OLD WOMAN: Got this friend. Should say, "I had this friend." Anyway . . . been friends since childhood. Could be sisters, we so much alike. Always like the same things. Same food. Same clothes. Same men . . . when we were young enough to do something 'bout it. Always like the same things. Even vote alike. Believe me, we seen a few presidents come and go. Lord . . . Didn't think we had the strength to go on when the ol' man die. Didn't like the idea of him cheatin' on ol' Eleanor. She weren't much to look at, that's true . . . but she was a carin' woman. However, he did have a hard life . . . bein' cripple and all. Maybe it was good he had a little forbidden fruit 'fore he left this earth. Always wondered how he did it with them braces and crutches. Then there was my Jack. Now, I never did care for his wife, but I loved that man . . . and my friend did, too. Anyway, she suppose to come over here today for tea. Both of us had this 'greement that if this one got back in the White House for four more years, we would both have tea and put poison in it and just check on outta here!

I can't stand him! Never was so good a actor 'till he start to mess with politics. I 'member him in the movies. Only two times I ever enjoy myself at one o' his flicks. First was when they cut off his legs in that picture where he was in love with Robert Cummings or somebody. Played that role and see how his son turn out? Pictures know, child! Pictures know! Second time was when he played in "The Killers." No, child. The remake! The remake! That's where he showed his true colors. Played the villain. He ordered the killing . . . just like he doin' now. Now he got four more years . . . and get in by a landslide . . . he gonna really show his behind. Don't give a damn 'bout nobody 'cept his rich friends. Every time I get ready to watch some of my programs on the teevee, here he come with some damn news conference. Then they got to hold up the program even more while some fool explain what he say. He don't mean nobody no good. Look how he call up that man with the fake heart and cause him to have a stroke 'cause he told him he was going to cut his Social Security. Had to flip-flop next day in the papers, but I betcha the man don't get his check. Oh, I was so glad they cut his legs off in "King's Row." Everytime it come on teevee, that's the only part I watch. If they had gone ahead and give him the 'cademy award for it, I might not be havin' this problem today. Anyway, my friend call me up and tell me . . . after she vote and all . . . she tell me she get in the booth and somethin' tell her to change her mind and vote for "him." Could hardly believe my ears. She say all of a sudden she start thinkin' 'bout what could happen if Mondale die or get bump off. She don't trust no woman bein' in charge of nothin' 'cause they too irrational. Can't argue with her there, 'cause she done prove her point when she change her vote! Plus, she say that would mean the Mafia be in control of the country. I had to remind her that even though my Jack was Catholic, the Pope didn't take over then . . . even 'though it look like he tryin' now . . . don't it? She come tellin' me the Mafia and Pope ain't the same. Know what I told her? I told her, "Hah!" Then she come tellin' me how Mondale don't look right. He do have this gangster face, I have to admit. Never will understand why when he had that little piece o' stuff done on his face, he didn't have his nose straightened all the way and did something 'bout that luggage he carrying under his eyes. She ain't entirely wrong when she say he don't look as healthy as this other one. I really ain't never seen Mondale doin' nothin' manly. This one always ridin' a horse or choppin' wood or pullin' in his stomach and stridin' like he a general or somethin' whenever he even see somebody with a movie camera. No wonder he fall 'sleep whenever he can. Did see Mondale in the rain, though. Cowboy and his lady don't never go out in the rain 'cause they 'fraid all that hair dye run down and turn the grass black and yellow. And speakin' o' that article, you see her lately? She ain't got much longer, I tell you! Ain't got no shoulders. Go straight from her neck to her waist. Straight up and down like six o'clock. Somethin' inside her havin' a good meal. Talk 'bout a woman being in charge. I told my friend that there's one in charge right now . . . 'cause she tell that fool the answer to all the questions . . . 'cause he can't hear 'em . . . even when he 'wake. I don't believe he was even shot that time. He just tryin' to look good to the people . . . like he some God . . . and can't die. Shoot, he ain't even show off his scars like Lyndon.

Then my friend come tellin' me she had a suspicion he was gonna win and she like to be on the winnin' side. I told her behine she black. She ain't never been on the winnin' side. Fool didn't want the black vote. He ain't go out and seek it. When last you hear tell of that? Sure knew how to grab them Pritty Ricans though. Put a few o' them in some little ass positions and got them thinking they white and American. Well, they ain't like bein' lump with us no how. Winnin' side? Hah! Honey, we ain't nothin' in this country now. Plus, she old. Old people ain't had no business votin' for that man. Lord, I bet he ain't nothin' but tubes and hernia 'neath them suits o' his. Well, I told her I ain't servin' her no poison tea 'cause I want her to live to regret what she done. I know I ain't drinkin' no poison-up tea 'cause I want to be here and see her regret what she done. I'm gonna tell her, "I told you so!" Everybody going to be sorry, believe me. Thought Hitler was bad? Hah! You ain't seen nothin' yet. Well, let me go watch my favorite movie on my VCR. "Casablanca"! It's my favorite 'cause he wasn't in it. He almost was, though. Can you see him instead of ol' Bogey? Yeah, he was almost in it, but them Warner Brothers knew something Annenberg and Gimbel didn't. See ya'll!

CURTAIN

www.ingramcontent.com/pod-product-compliance
Lightning Source LLC
Chambersburg PA
CBHW060545100426

42742CB00013B/2457